Problem Regions of Europe
General Editor: **D. I. Scargill**

The Moscow City Region
F. E. Ian Hamilton

Oxford University Press 1976

Oxford University Press, Ely House, London W.1

Oxford London Glasgow New York Toronto Melbourne
Wellington Cape Town Ibadan Nairobi Dar es Salaam Lusaka
Addis Ababa Kuala Lumpur Singapore Jakarta Hong Kong
Tokyo Delhi Bombay Calcutta Madras Karachi

I would like to thank Mrs. Janet Baker of the
Drawing Office, the London School of
Economics, for preparing the maps.
F.E.I.H.

Filmset by BAS Printers Limited, Wallop, Hampshire
and printed in Great Britain
at the University Press, Oxford
by Vivian Ridler, Printer to the University

Editor's Preface

Great economic and social changes have taken place in Europe in recent years. The agricultural workforce in the west was halved, for example, during the 1950s and 1960s. This unprecedented flight from the land has made possible some much-needed reorganization of farm holdings but it has also created problems, not least that of finding uses for land in the highlands and elsewhere where it is no longer profitable to farm. Closely related is the difficulty of maintaining services to a much diminished rural population or of providing new kinds of services for the holidaymakers who increasingly buy up rural properties.

Contraction of the labour force has also taken place in many traditional industries. The coal-mining industry alone has shed two-thirds of its workforce since 1950. The resulting problems have been especially serious in those mining or manufacturing districts which have a high level of dependence on a single source of employment—a not uncommon result of Europe's industrial past—and the efforts of those who seek to attract new industries are often thwarted by a legacy of pollution, bad housing, and soured labour relations.

Quite a different set of problems has arisen in the great cities of Europe such as London and Paris and in the conurbations of closely linked cities well exemplified by Randstad Holland. Here are problems due to growth brought about by the expansion of consumer-orientated manufacturing and still more by the massive increase in office jobs which proliferate in 'down-town' business districts. The problems are economic, social and political, and they include the effects of congestion, of soaring land values, of the increasing divorce of place of residence from place of work, and of the difficulty of planning a metropolitan region that may be shared between many independent-minded local authorities.

The problems resulting from change are not passing ones; indeed they exhibit a persistence that amply justifies their study on an areal basis. Hence the *Problem Regions of Europe* series. The volumes in the series have all been written by geographers who, by the nature of their discipline, can take a broadly based approach to description and analysis. Geographers in the past have been reluctant to base their studies on problem regions since the problem was often of a temporary nature, less enduring than the 'personality' of the region but the magnitude of present-day problems has even resulted in the suggestion that regions should be defined in terms of the problems that confront them.

Certain themes emerge clearly when the basis of the problem is examined: the effects of a harsh environment, of remoteness and of political division, as well as of industrial decay or urban congestion. But these have not been examined in isolation and the studies that make up the series have been carefully chosen in order that useful comparisons can be made. Thus, for example, both the Mezzogiorno and Andalusia have to contend with the problems of Mediterranean drought, wind, and flood, but the precise nature of these and other problems, as well as man's response to them, differs in the two regions. Similarly, the response to economic change is not the same in North-East England as in North Rhine–Westphalia, nor the response to social pressures the same in Paris as in the Randstad.

The efforts which individual governments have made to grapple with their problems provides a basis for critical assessment in each of the volumes. For too long, solutions were sought that were piecemeal and short-term. Our own Development Areas in Britain provide a good illustration of this kind of policy. Of late, however, European governments have shown an increasing awareness of the need to undertake planning on a regional basis. The success or otherwise of such regional policies is fully explored in the individual *Problem Region* volumes.

When it was first planned the *Problem Region* series was thought of as useful only to the sixth-form student of geography. As it has developed it has become clear that the authors—all specialists in the geography of the areas concerned—have contributed studies that will be useful, not only for sixth-form work, but as a basis for the more detailed investigations undertaken by advanced students, both of geography and of European studies in general.

D.I.S.

St. Edmund Hall, Oxford

3

Contents

1　The Soviet Background

The Soviet economic, military, political, and social challenge is strong, yet detailed study of the U.S.S.R. is limited. The region of its capital, Moscow, is among the areas of Europe most neglected in geographical research. Distance partly explains this, so does the abysmally limited learning of the Russian language. Serious scholarly study at the regional scale is also severely constrained, however, by gaps in Soviet information sources. Yet the Moscow city region demonstrates problems and processes which are both similar to, and distinct from, those of other European metropolitan regions. Similarities consist in the containment of metropolitan growth. Differences lie in the operation of wide-ranging, changing, and conflicting Soviet planning strategies during the sixty years since the October Revolution of 1917. Planning decisions involve the selection and ranking of priorities for the use of the scarce resources of time, money, materials and people. In the centrally-planned Soviet economy, priorities are ranked for the entire State and its regions. Low priorities of one planning period often become nationwide or regional problems requiring remedies in subsequent planning periods. Thus the city region illustrates how planning strategies and processes may generate urban and regional problems—particularly under conditions of forced economic growth—and how counter measures have been introduced to solve these problems.

The U.S.S.R. is a multi-national state, a union comprising fifteen Soviet socialist republics (S.S.R.s). Of these, the Russian Soviet Federal Socialist Republic (R.S.F.S.R.) is by far the largest and most populous and influential (Table 1). Yet Russians form only 53 per cent of Soviet population; the remainder comprises 107 quite distinct non-Russian nationalities, including Ukrainians (41 million), Uzbeks (9), Belorussians (9).

The Ural Mountains, a north–south ridge some 2500 km long, divide the U.S.S.R. into a western 'European' part and an eastern 'Asiatic' part. Moscow is situated centrally in the European U.S.S.R., which embraces one-fourth of Soviet territory, approximately five million km². Larger than Eastern and Western Europe combined, this is the key economic zone of the Soviet Union and of Comecon. It accounts for three-quarters of the Soviet people (42 per cent are non-Russians) and of industrial output and freight movements, and two-thirds of farm output. Resources, though limited as a proportion of overall Soviet totals, are large by European standards. Timber, fur and amber from the north, grain from the south-central blackearth zone, coal and iron from the Donbass in the south, oil from the Caspian Sea and Volga regions, diverse minerals from the Urals—these sources of wealth have sustained eight centuries of Russian Imperial territorial expansion before 1900 and part of Soviet economic expansion after 1917.

TABLE 1

Some indices of the world significance of the U.S.S.R., 1972 (all figures in millions)

	Area (km²)	Population	Coal	Oil	Steel (tonnes)	Grains	Vehicles (units)
			Production				
U.S.S.R.	22·42	247·5	450	394	126	158	1·4
of which : R.S.F.S.R.	*17·07*	*131·9*	*355*	*306*	*69*	*113*	*1·1*
Eastern Europe	1·33	127·3	191	20	48	84	1·1
Western Europe*	3·59	341·5	265	10	149	126	12·1
Canada	9·98	21·8	19	67	12	33	1·5
U.S.A.	9·36	208·8	517	468	120	205	11·5
China	9·60	800·7	434	32	22	189	0·04
India	3·27	563·5	74	7	7	95	0·06
Japan	0·37	105·9	29	0	93	16	6·1

*The E.E.C. States and Finland, Greece, Iceland, Norway, Portugal, Spain, Sweden, and Switzerland.

2 The Moscow City Region: An Introduction

The Moscow region itself shares few of these resources directly. Indeed, nature endowed it poorly. Why, then, is Moscow the centre of a major metropolitan region? The answer lies in its supreme spatial nodality. The city owes its emergence as the military, trading and, later, industrial pivot of the State to the skill with which successive Russian and later Soviet rulers have exploited its nodality (Fig. 1) to develop and to maintain the centralization of administrative power. Once firmly established, political centrality became self-perpetuating by endowing Moscow and its region with the comparative advantage of economic centrality. Until 1850, nodality was vested in the use of a primary river system linked by secondary roads. These gave Muscovites access to most of Europe and the Baltic and Black Seas. After 1850, nodality was made supreme by the progressive State development of radial railway, road, waterway, air, electric power and pipeline links which focus on the city: the metropolitan region has the densest communications network in the entire U.S.S.R.

Some European comparisons

In function, layout, even appearance, Moscow distils the essence of many other European capitals. Set amid the forests, lakes, marshlands and poor soils of the Russian plain, devoid of significant resources, and yet transformed by man into a powerful State-unifying force, Moscow exhibits strong historic parallels with Berlin. The Kremlin (Russian *Kreml'*: a fortified settlement), symbol of defence and military power, reminds one of the Imperial legacies in Rome. The modern ring boulevards, built on former defences, and the radial thoroughfares which transect the boulevards in all directions are reminiscent of Paris.

With 7·4 million people living within the city's administrative area (886 km²) in 1975, Moscow clearly ranks with London and Paris as one of the 'big three' European capitals. It dominates a highly urbanized area which contains forty-eight vigorously expanding towns with populations between 16 000 and 175 000, within 70 km of the Kremlin. This *Moscow metropolitan area* houses some 10·5–11 million people and is comparable in size and shape to the London metropolitan planning region. Size and importance are interrelated, yet even the metropolitan area is an inadequate measure of the tremendous importance of Moscow. The city performs major roles on five geographic levels as: centre of the metropolitan region, capital of the R.S.F.S.R., capital and principal city of the Soviet Union, headquarters of Comecon, and world city.

The relative significance of the functions of the city change with scale. Cultural and economic roles broadly dominate the region. Up the hierarchical scale the political functions of this centre of Soviet policy-making and administration, and of a world Communist movement, progressively take precedence. Moscow cannot boast a Stock Exchange like London, yet there is far-reaching economic significance in the decisions concerning Soviet and Comecon trade with the non-Communist world, financial and technical aid to developing countries, international container-traffic facilities via the Trans-Siberian railway, or fishing limits. As the political and economic centre of Comecon and the Warsaw Treaty Organization, Moscow performs for the socialist world those functions which, in Western Europe, are divided between Brussels as the headquarters of the E.E.C. and Nato, and Paris as headquarters of the O.E.C.D. Such dominance results as much from the city's world political role as from its being the leading Soviet financial, manufacturing, trading, cultural, and scientific centre.

Unquestionably, Moscow is primate city of the U.S.S.R., though less dominant than Paris in France or Budapest in Hungary. Within 700 km of Moscow lie four major Soviet urban complexes: Leningrad (4 million inhabitants), Kiev (1·8 million), Gorky (1·5 million), and Kharkov (1·3 million). Another eleven, each housing 1 to 1·5 million people, are dispersed throughout the country: four in the Donbass industrial and Black Sea areas (Donetsk-Makayevka, Dniepropetrovsk, Rostov-on-Don, and Odessa), the remainder being major industrial nodes (Baku, Kuybyshev, Sverdlovsk, Chelyabinsk, and Novosibirsk) or republic capitals (Tashkent and Tbilisi).

Moscow was not always primate city. Kiev was the capital of the ancient Russian State from 882 to 1169. For the next 200 years, political fragmentation stifled the emergence of any politically-supreme town, though Novgorod led in trade and handicrafts. Moscow was the capital of a reunified

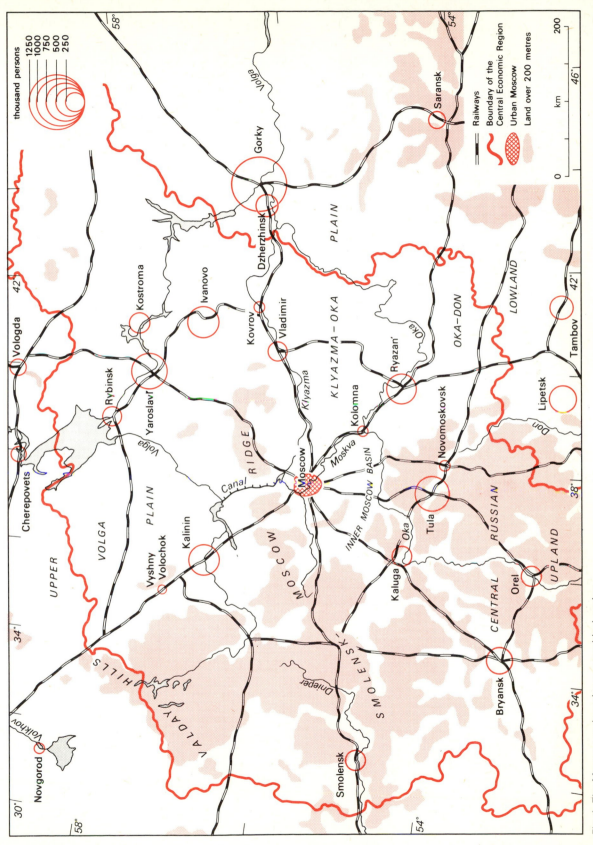

Fig. 1. The Moscow region: the geographical setting

Reservoirs on rivers and canals enhance the beauty and recreational value of the Forest Park Belt around Moscow and attract three million visitors at weekends

Fig. 2. The administrative and planning framework: *oblasts* of the Central Region and neighbouring economic regions

and expanding Russian State from 1380 until 1712 when Peter the Great created a new capital in Petersburg (now Leningrad). Overseas trading, shipping industries, and the administration of an expanding continental Empire stimulated the rapid growth of Petersburg before 1914, and the initial advantage gained then sustained further economic expansion of Leningrad after the Revolution.

Large-scale exploitation of vast, diverse and dispersed natural resources for industry explains the growth of the continental interior cities of the Donbass, Volga basin, Urals, and Siberia. That three leading Soviet cities (Kiev, Tashkent, and Tbilisi) are republic capitals, however, underlines the importance of decentralized regional administration as a force in the planned economic growth of areas inhabited by non-Russian nationalities. Though the politico-economic power centralized in Moscow exceeds that localized in Paris (because of much greater Soviet size, economic status, and centralized planning), the extent of decentralized planning within the Soviet federal structure endows non-Russian administrations in republic capitals with more influence over the development and location of regional economic activities than is the case in French provincial cities.

Definition of the city region

Lying within the extensive Russian forest belt amid the vast, gently undulating east European plain, the Moscow region displays few marked landforms. Slight variations in environment result from latitudinal climatic differences rather than from relief. The physical environment is poor—historically one of refuge rather than attraction—but nature herself poses few problems to the region compared with those challenging Soviet man in huge areas of the harsh Arctic northlands and north-eastern Siberia, in the Pripet or West Siberian marshlands, and in the semi-arid steppe and arid deserts of the south-centre.

Such environmental problems as do exist stem (as with most other problems) from the speed, scale and substance of the urbanization and industrialization processes emanating from the metropolitan core. Thus, in the Moscow city region are manifested those problems resulting from dominantly metropolitan processes, and the planning policies employed to remedy those problems. Defined in this way, it approximates to the Central Region (*Tsentral'ny Rayon*), one of the nineteen economic planning regions into which the U.S.S.R. is divided. The Central Region (Fig. 2) comprises twelve administrative districts (*oblasts*): Moscow city is a separate entity at its heart. Soviet geographers believe, on grounds of Marxist-Leninist dialectic materialism, that regions really exist because their functional characteristics are created and fashioned by State planning decisions. For them the economic planning region is the unit of regional description. A rigid definition of the Moscow city region as the Central Region would, therefore, be entirely in the Soviet tradition.

Yet many problems occur within 70 km of the Kremlin while others extend to, or only appear towards, the periphery and require planning solutions linked to those of neighbouring economic planning regions: the Northwest (centre: Leningrad), Volga-Vyatka (centre: Gorky), and Central Chernozem (centre: Voronezh). This is inevitable. Oriented south-west to north-east, the Central Region cuts across the periphery of a remarkable ring/radial transport network which focuses upon Moscow. Indeed, this network binds the city region together into one functional system. Though periodic changes have been made to the Central Region's boundaries, key sections of the outer transport ring lie outside it: Cherepovets—Vologda (Northwest), Gorky—Arzamas—Saransk (Volga-Vyatka), the Penza (Volga region: *Povol'zhe*), and Tambov—Lipetsk—Yelets (Central Chernozem) sections. These form the outer limits of the Moscow city region to the north, east and south respectively; the Central Region incorporates the western boundaries.

Defined thus the Moscow city region is as large as France (about 550 000 km²) and contains 40 million people, of whom 22 million live in 180 towns and cities. Though extensive, it displays all the features of a city region. The integrative role of the transport system is fundamental. For Soviet planning it operates simultaneously as (i) a powerful centripetal economic, psychological and social force which encourages the concentration in Moscow and its immediate hinterland of people, housing, jobs, social and decision-making contacts; and (ii) a centrifugal force providing the means for channelling growth away from the capital into many nodal sub-regional centres to offset the disadvantages of metropolitan congestion. Radial and ring routes shape the physical pattern of the city region: the spread of Moscow, the overspill of her population into rows of satellite towns along most of the radial routes, and the spacing of urban centres of local *rayon*, subregional *oblast*, and industrial importance throughout the region.

The city region is economically complex. Varying degrees of urbanization associated with industrial and metropolitan growth are superimposed on significant areal specialization of rural land-uses based on soil differences. But it is through specialization in manufacturing that the urban clusters centred on Moscow, Tula, and the upper Volga river have made their biggest contribution to its pre-eminence as the 'central industrial region'. Indeed, major problems stem from its success in innovating, manufacturing, and supplying to other regions the sophisticated equipment and articles of mass consumption required by planned development. Economically, too, the region is unusual in the U.S.S.R. for its very high dependence on raw materials and energy inputs from outside its territory.

People in the city region are bound together by an awareness of common interests. For most citizens of the metropolitan area, Moscow provides employment, education, entertainment, culture, and services. Common interests are hardly less strong throughout Moscow *oblast* which is administratively dependent upon the metropolis, its agriculture dominated by the demand for perishable vegetables and milk, and increasingly affected by activities decentralized from the capital. Beyond, unity finds expression in the co-operation between the twelve *oblasts* and Moscow city in planning, administering, and solving the problems of the Central Region.

The speed and scale of metropolitan growth since 1920 has drawn thousands of migrants annually to Moscow and its satellite towns from the entire Central Region and neighbouring areas of European Russia, the Ukraine, and Belorussia. Today, electrified railways put most within five or six hours' travel time of their families and friends, permitting regular social contacts throughout the region, and creating strong social cohesion. Yet the region is constantly changing. High occupational mobility of its people is interrelated with their geographic mobility. Population censuses of 1926, 1959, and 1970 show movement on two planes: (i) inter-regionally, people move into the city region, replacing others who accept the challenge of life elsewhere; and (ii) intra-regionally, they gravitate to Moscow, replacing those who move out into Moscow *oblast* or beyond. As the Soviet economy grows, regional functions alter in composition and importance, requiring both new locations for new activities and the locational rearrangement of existing activities.

Regional characteristics

Moscow lies towards the centre of a Tertiary basin, which shares common features with the London and Paris basins. Yet the Moscow basin is quite distinctive. An extensive Quaternary glacial

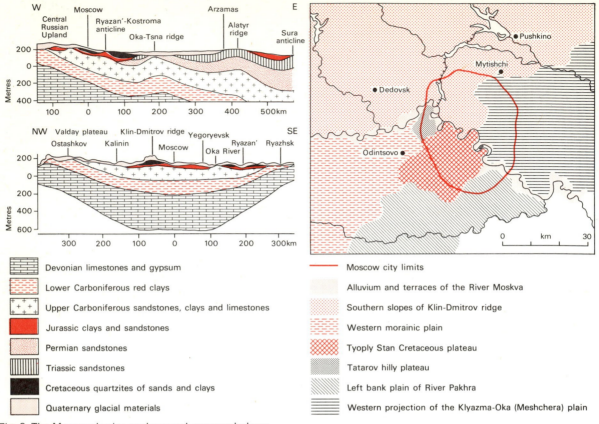

Fig. 3. The Moscow basin: geology and geomorphology

Legend (left):
- Devonian limestones and gypsum
- Lower Carboniferous red clays
- Upper Carboniferous sandstones, clays and limestones
- Jurassic clays and sandstones
- Permian sandstones
- Triassic sandstones
- Cretaceous quartzites of sands and clays
- Quaternary glacial materials

Legend (right):
- Moscow city limits
- Alluvium and terraces of the River Moskva
- Southern slopes of Klin-Dmitrov ridge
- Western morainic plain
- Tyoply Stan Cretaceous plateau
- Tatarov hilly plateau
- Left bank plain of River Pakhra
- Western projection of the Klyazma-Oka (Meshchera) plain

cover mantles most of the region—moraine, outwash sands, boulder, and interglacial lacustrine clays—burying successive synclinal strata of Cretaceous, Jurassic, Carboniferous, and Devonian age which are gently uptilted westwards (Fig. 3). Where these outcrop they elevate the glacial cover into hilly plateau-like elevations which rise to 275–320 m (cf. Moscow 125–150 m) forming the Valday hills in the north-west and the Central Russian uplands in the south. Bisecting the basin in a south-west to north-east direction, just north of Moscow, is the Smolensk–Moscow (Klin-Dmitrov) ridge, the southernmost terminal moraine of maximum glaciation, which overlays a ridge of Cretaceous strata (Fig. 4). A 'prong' of this ridge slopes south-eastwards to the very heart of the metropolis, disappearing under the terraces of the Moskva river at the Kremlin. An outlier, the Tyoply Stan upland, is represented by the Lenin hills just below Moscow State University (M.G.U.: Moskovsky Gosudarstvenny Universitet), exposing Cretaceous quartzite sands capped by interglacial clays and moraine.

The city region today extends beyond the western hill rim around Bryansk and far out eastwards into the Oka-Volga plains. That it does so demonstrates the advantages to Muscovites of easy access by land and water in all directions through the low arc-like watershed of the Valday hills, Smolensk ridge, and Central uplands. Here rise all the great rivers of the European U.S.S.R., the mighty Volga and its tributaries (Moskva, Klyazma and Oka); the Dnieper, Desna and Don; the Dvina and Volkhov. Nodality is combined with contrasting physical environments which offer complementary economic opportunities within the region. The city thus became the hub of regional commerce, contacts, handicrafts, and areal specialization.

Simply stated, Moscow lies between hills and plateaux to the west, and low-lying plains to the east of a line drawn approximately through Vyshny Volochok, Ryazan', and Lipetsk; between a cooler, wetter, dominantly coniferous forest belt, developed on poor acidic podsols to the north, and a warmer, drier, dominantly deciduous forest belt, developed on the more fertile grey-forest soils to the south of a Bryansk–Gorky line. This southern zone rapidly grades into rich *chernozem* (black-earth) steppe.

In fact, the city region comprises six distinctive sub-regions. The *north-western plateau* (the Valday hills and Smolensk ridge) is a drier, rolling hill area with poor morainic soils which are heavily forested and offer limited farming opportunities. Flax, rye and potatoes are grown, as are pasture and fodder for livestock fattening. To the north-east lies the *Upper Volga plain*, an area with abundant surface water, marsh and forest. Dairying, potatoes and rye are significant in less waterlogged or sandy areas, but the Volga river has long stimulated urban manufacturing in the Ivanovo/Yaroslavl' area using imported materials. South of Moscow rise the *Central Russian uplands*. The expansive rolling relief resembles the Smolensk ridge, but the landscapes are otherwise quite different. Lying mostly southward of the glaciated zone, in a warmer climate, the Central uplands are under far more arable cultivation—of wheat and sugar-beet rather than potatoes, with oats and rye as the grey-forest soils grade into the *chernozem* belt. Forests often remain as farmland shelter belts rather than as timber stands. Around Tula and Novomoskovsk occurs the only important industrial resource of the city region: brown coal. Just beyond, in the Central Chernozem Region, lie the huge iron ore reserves of the Kursk 'magnetic anomaly'. To the east and south-east lie two adjoining lowlands. The *Klyazma-Oka (or Meshchera) plain* is very marshy, like the Upper Volga plain, but more transitional between the sub-regions of coniferous forest/podsol and the deciduous forest/grey-forest soil. Extensive peat deposits around Shatura (120 km east of Moscow) and Gorky provide a limited local energy base. The *Oka-Don lowland*, a watershed zone, is drier, fertile and, like the blackearth area, highly cultivated.

These sub-regions surround the *Inner Moscow basin*, the physical, social, and economic hub of the entire city region. It distils the physical essence of the surrounding sub-regions: western hills and eastern plains meet in central Moscow (Figs. 3 and 4). Apart from plentiful building materials, the only significant resource is the phosphate deposit near Voskresensk. With its transport network, the Inner Moscow basin links the economies of all the sub-regions, concentrates the densest population, and, in the metropolitan area, exhibits the greatest alteration by man of the physical environment.

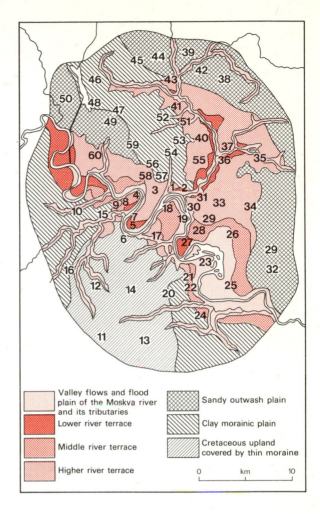

Valley flows and flood plain of the Moskva river and its tributaries	Sandy outwash plain
Lower river terrace	Clay morainic plain
Middle river terrace	Cretaceous upland covered by thin moraine
Higher river terrace	0 km 10

Fig. 4. Geomorphological zones of Moscow city

1 Kremlin
2 Rossiya hotel
3 Kalinin Prospekt
4 Hotel Ukraina
5 Lenin Stadium
6 Moscow State University
7 Novodevichy Monastery
8 Kutuzovsky Prospekt
9 Borodino
10 Kuntsevo
11 Tyoply Stan
12 Yugo-Zapadnaya metro
13 Chertanovo
14 Kaluzhkaya metro
15 Moskva-Sortirovochnaya
16 Ochakovo
17 Donskoi Monastery
18 Paveletsky terminus
19 Paveletsky terminus
20 Varshavskaya metro

21 Sadovniki
22 Kolomenskoye Monastery
23 Nagatino
24 Tsaritsyno station
25 Lyublino
26 Tekstil'shchiki
27 Avtozavodskaya
28 Novostanovskaya street
29 Volgograd Prospekt
30 Novospassky Monastery
31 Andrei Rublev Monastery
32 Kuzminki forest
33 Serp i Molot
34 Perovo
35 Izmailovskaya metro
36 Elektrozavodskaya metro
37 Preobrazhenskaya metro
38 Kuybyshev forest
39 Medvedkovo
40 Sokolniki

41 V.D.N.H.
42 Babushkin
43 Ostradnoye
44 Beskudnikovo
45 Degunino
46 Khimki-Khovrino
47 Timiryazev park
48 Vodny Stadion
49 Sokol metro
50 Tushino
51 Shcherbakovskaya
52 Ostankino
53 Riga terminus
54 Soviet Army park
55 Krasnoselskaya metro
56 Belorussky terminus
57 Gorky street
58 Krasnopresnenskaya metro
59 Leningradsky Prospekt
60 Khoroshevskaya 3rd street

3 Problems Through Time

Problems vary through time in character, in magnitude, and in the significance attached to them. The growth of Moscow, at times considered necessary, has been seen at other times as undesirable. So, too, has the lag in agriculture, which restricted supplies of food to the cities, whilst simultaneously depressing rural standards and encouraging cityward population migration. Other problems are temporal, amenable to short-term solution, but may be succeeded by new difficulties. Industrialization replaced the economic backwardness and overpopulation of the Tsarist era by increasing the scarcities of natural resources and labour, imposing pressures on the environment and deepening the complexities of planning and managing an ever-expanding metropolitan core.

Environmental problems

Historically, the physical problems in the north and east resembled those of the neighbouring lowland glacial areas in Belorussia, around Petersburg, Pskov, and Novgorod. Marshland reclamation and soil improvement were essential to sustain a rapidly growing peasant population practising primitive farm techniques.

After 1917 new environmental problems resulted from massive industrialization. First, 5 per cent of regional farm and forest land disappeared, mainly under reservoirs created to supply water to hydro-electric power barrages and to cities. The Rybinsk reservoir on the Volga river, the third largest artificial lake in the U.S.S.R., flooded 415 000 ha of farm and forest land alone—equivalent to the Lower Rhône region of France—and required the relocation of 500 settlements. Other reservoirs near Gorky and Moscow have doubled the area lost. These losses, small in percentage terms, are significant regionally because the fresh food supplies to Moscow are inadequate and the mature forest resources in the south are nearly exhausted from overcutting in the area between Bryansk, Kursk, Tambov, and Moscow.

Secondly, pressures exist on the quantity and the quality of regional water supplies, despite the great rivers and artesian water in aquifers under the Inner Moscow basin. Currently Moscow consumes twice as much water daily as Greater London. Artesian water beneath the Soviet capital is now 35–40 m below its 1917 level, the water table throughout the city region, 3–4 m lower. As the costs of extracting diminishing reserves from its 700 artesian wells rise, Moscow consumes more water from the rivers Moskva, Klyazma, and especially the Upper Volga (via the Ivan'kovo reservoir and Moscow canal).

Thirdly, environmental pollution is serious. City sewage and effluent from cellulose-paper, oil refinery, chemical, textile, metallurgical, and metal-working industries make the Volga, Oka, Moskva, Klyazma, Dnieper, Desna, Uvod and Upa rivers among the forty most polluted rivers in the U.S.S.R. Not only does river pollution raise technical and economic problems of purification and recycling, it also filters into groundwater systems and adversely affects agriculture. Urban nodes also create air pollution, but this is far less grim than in the Donbass, Urals, or Kuzbass industrial regions.

Extensive lowland, however, poses obstacles neither to airborne pollution nor to extensive land inundation by new reservoirs. Rivers transport the pollutants into neighbouring drier regions which are crucial to Soviet agriculture and which depend upon river-water supply: the northern Ukraine, the blackearth area, and the Volga basin. The effects are thus inter-regional as well as regional—the more so as Soviet decision-makers 'think big', conceiving multi-purpose river schemes and industrial complexes or planning solutions to metropolitan agglomeration on a very broad scale. This creates conflicts between the existing and potential alternative uses of land in the city region, the most densely-populated and urbanized region in the U.S.S.R.

Economic and social problems

Although the city region could support small-scale industry from its own resources, the rapid and diversified industrialization after 1928 created an insatiable regional demand for energy and minerals. It led to the intensified resource extraction of low-quality local resources at high cost, and progressively greater dependence upon cheaper, better-quality supplies transported over increasing distances.

Even great expansion of regional energy production could not cope with the sharply and continually increasing demand. Brown-coal output, mainly around Tula, was raised from less than 1 million tonnes in 1928 to almost 50 million tonnes in 1958, but has since stabilized at around 40 million tonnes in the face of more efficient natural gas supplies. Successive downstream construction (1934–56) created the upper Volga cascade of H.E.P. stations at Ivan'kovo, Uglich, Rybinsk, and Zavol'zhe (near Gorky). Before Stalin's death in 1953, most of the supplies for industry came from the Donbass (coal, iron ore, steel), Baku (oil), Central Asia (cotton), and the North-west (timber). Since then, supplies have been drawn increasingly from the Kola peninsula (iron ore and other minerals), Carpathians (gas), Volga/Urals (electricity, oil, gas, metals, chemical raw materials), North Caucasus (gas), West Siberia (oil, timber), whilst semi-manufactured goods are imported from many regions including the Comecon partners in Eastern Europe.

Such dependence creates innumerable problems. Regional imports normally exceed exports by one-third to a half, burdening inter-regional transport. Production costs often exceed those in other regions, most noticeably before 1960 when railways hauled most of the incoming freight and congestion caused frequent delays. Since then, the construction of gas and oil pipelines and high-tension electricity lines has alleviated this pressure, reduced the cost of energy supplies and stimulated continued growth in the Moscow city

TABLE 2

Population changes in the Moscow city region, 1940–70

Economic regions	Oblasts in the city region	Population (thousands)			Percentage changes 1959–70		
		1940	1959	1970	Total	Urban	Rural
Northwest		*11 204*	*10 865*	*12 157*	*+12*	*+27*	*−15*
	Vologda†		1309	1296	−1	+36	−20
*Central**		*27 044*	*25 718*	*27 659*	*+7·5*	*+29*	*−24*
	Bryansk†		1550	1582	+2	+39	−17
	Ivanovo		1320	1339	+1	+15	−26
	Kalinin		1805	1717	−5	+24	−27
	Kaluga		939	995	+6	+47	−18
	Kostroma		921	871	−5·5	+27	−27
	Moscow city		6044	7061	+17	—	—
	Moscow *oblast*		4906	5775	+18	+44	−16
	Orel†		929	931	+0·2	+64	−20
	Ryazan'†		1445	1412	−2	+53	−26
	Smolensk†		1141	1106	−3	+45	−26
	Tula		1919	1953	+2	+20	−26
	Vladimir		1406	1512	+7	+28	−20
	Yaroslavl'		1396	1400	+0·3	+21	−28
*Volga-Vyatka**		*8848*	*8252*	*8348*	*+1*	*+37*	*−22*
	Gorky		3618	3683	+2	+26	−25
	Mordov A.S.S.R.†		1002	1030	+3	+103	−20
*Central Chernozem**		*9093*	*7769*	*7998*	*+3*	*+52*	*−15*
	Kursk†		1483	1474	−1	+60	−16
	Lipetsk†		1142	1224	+7	+57	−14
	Tambov†		1549	1512	−2	+45	−19
	Voronezh†		2367	2527	+7	+40	−11
Volga		*15 649*	*15 975*	*18 373*	*+15*	*+43*	*−8*
	Penza		1508	1536	+2	+36	−15
Total (city region)			39 696	41 934	10·5	+31	−21
Total (three economic regions)*		44 985	41 739	44 005	10·5	+32·5	−21

†*Oblasts* in which rural population still exceeds urban population.

Sources: Itogi Vsesoyuznoi Perepisi Naseleniya 1970 goda, Tom. I, Moscow 1972; *Yubileyny Statisticheski Yezhegodnik Narodnoye Khozyaystvo, S.S.S.R., 1922–72,* Moscow 1972.

region. Coming at a time when economic re-organization has increased State concern for efficiency, this trend has posed new dilemmas for planners long committed to a policy of inter-regional industrial dispersion based upon local (in Soviet terms, regional) use of resources. The execution of such a policy in the past has, in fact, required a continual redistribution of capital from the city region, the effect of which has been not so much to restrict economic growth as to hinder the adequate provision and modernization of a social infrastructure, especially housing.

Not least among current economic problems is an acute labour shortage which, though a recent phenomenon, is the cumulative result of two persistently divergent trends since 1913: slow population growth and rapid expansion in demand for labour.

The three economic regions that Moscow dominates—the Central, Central Chernozem, and Volga-Vyatka—recorded the lowest population increases in the entire U.S.S.R. between 1959 and 1970 (Fig. 5). Indeed, fewer people (Table 2) lived there in 1970 (44 005 000) than in 1940 (44 985 000), but more than in 1959 (41 739 000). These facts reflect the unhappy social history of the western U.S.S.R. since 1913. Estimates put total losses at 50 million dead: 15 million during the First World War, October Revolution, and Civil War period; 5 million during farm collectivization (1931–3); 30 million in the Second World War. As a result, the Moscow city region currently has a *natural* shortfall of 5–10 million people. An abnormally large excess of women over men greatly restricted wartime and post-war marriages and births. Currently, working people aged 20–35 and 45–54 are exceptionally scarce. Women form 56 per cent of the labour force employed in Moscow and Moscow *oblast*: 30 per cent of all transport and construction workers are women, as are 53 per cent in manufacturing, 60 per cent in administration, 68 per cent in social services, and 80 per cent in retail services.

This situation contrasts starkly with Moscow in the 1870s when men outnumbered women by 3:2, a social imbalance which added to the frustrations of poor living and working conditions. Since 1945, population imbalance, combined with Soviet policy to weaken the family as a social unit, has contributed to a soaring divorce rate second only to that in the U.S.A.

Regional labour scarcity has been aggravated by the direct and indirect effects of Soviet policy. Maintenance of a huge Red Army, reported in 1975 to number 3 425 000 men (equal to 7·5 per cent of the civilian male labour force) has lasting effects. Control over labour mobility using domestic passports and residence registration is intended

Fig. 5. Recent Soviet regional population trends. (a) Indices of growth 1959–70. (b) Sources of net migration gains and losses in the Central Region 1968–9

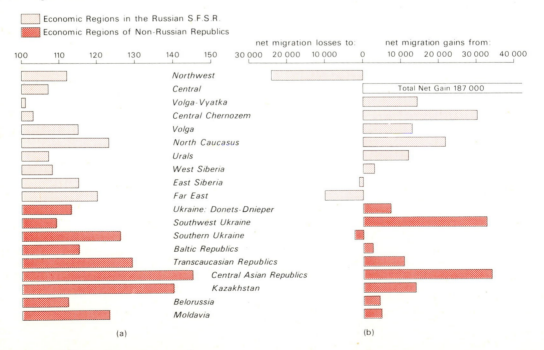

(a)   (b)

to discourage migration into Moscow and to stimulate out-migration to Kazakhstan, Siberia and the Far East. Acute urban housing shortages and the high proportion of working women have dramatically reduced the birth-rate, lowering the rate of natural increase despite a decreased mortality rate. Natural increase in the R.S.F.S.R. dropped from 17 per 1000 in 1950 (birth-rate 27, death-rate 10) to under 6 in 1970 (birth-rate 15, death-rate 9). Corresponding rates were far lower in Moscow, declining from 7 (birth-rate 15, death-rate 8) to only 2·5 (birth-rate 12, death-rate 9·5).

The enormous socio-economic attraction of Moscow as a place in which to live and work continues, creating practical difficulties for Soviet labour policy implementation, housing supply and, potentially, long-term social problems. Despite restrictions, net migration into the Central Region continues (Fig. 5) being 187 000 in 1968–9, according to the 1970 Census, 60 per cent of them (121 000 people) net migrants into Moscow alone. If this rate is representative for the entire intercensal period 1959–70, net gains from interregional migration account for 50 per cent of the city/regional and 66 per cent of Moscow city population increases. Indeed, the Central Region (Fig. 5) has positive migration balances (i.e. net gains) with fourteen Soviet economic regions, negative balances with only four. Most net in-migration (70 per cent) is from dominantly or partly non-Russian inhabited regions where population growth rates exceed the Soviet average (Fig. 5); only 30 per cent from adjacent Central Chernozem, Volga-Vyatka, and Volga regions. Many of the migrants are non-Russians for, apart from inflows of temporary foreign workers from other East European Comecon nations, they alone can fill the regional labour supply gap. The number of non-Russians living and working in Moscow has risen rapidly from 380 000 (6·3 per cent) in 1959 to 759 760 (10·8 per cent) in 1970. Yet two-thirds of net in-migration still came from within 1000 km of the capital.

The major social problem since 1917 has been where and how to house the continual flows of migrants who gravitate to the metropolis. From 1920 to 1960 population growth in the capital (from 1·8 to 6·2 million) far outstripped increases in housing supply, resulting in overcrowding and decreased per capita living space compared with 1913 (Fig. 6). On the regional scale, divergent yet closely interrelated population trends are evident (Table 2). First, stagnation or decline occurred in fifteen peripheral *oblasts*. Collectively, they lost 1·1 million people (5 per cent) between 1959 and 1970. Secondly, increasing concentration occurred in

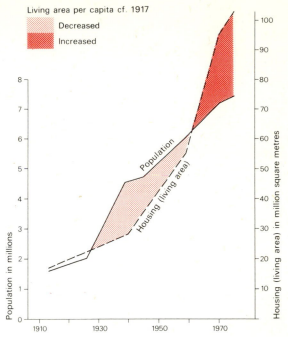

Fig. 6. Population growth and housing supply in Moscow city, 1913–75

the centre where only Moscow city and *oblast* recorded large increases (17-18 per cent), though growth did 'overspill' east into Vladimir and south-west into Kaluga *oblasts*: population here rose from 13·3 million to 15·3 million. Only the Voronezh-Lipetsk zones in the periphery recorded significant population growth (7 per cent). Rural areas generally lost 15–28 per cent of their population to the cities, and urbanization was more rapid in the rural south.

Before the October Revolution

The transfer of the Imperial capital to Petersburg in 1713 brought about fifty years of economic depression in the Moscow region. No railways existed before 1851, making the continental interior less competitive than Petersburg which lay on the Neva and was open to world sea routes. Feudalism polarized a dominantly rural society into a few aristocratic rich and a mass of wretched serfs, restricting markets, capital supply and economic expansion. Two developments altered the situation: emancipation of the serfs (1861) increased labour mobility and the 'railway boom' (1860–90) increased goods mobility. Moscow used its continued financial supremacy over Petersburg to become a railway focus, attracting industry and thousands of peasants in search of work. New problems emerged: rapid urban growth, an unhealthy male : female population ratio and overcrowded living conditions, the worst found in the

24 500 'coop-cell' tenements (*koyechno-kamorochnykh kvartir*) housing 325 000 workers.

Development under Lenin and Stalin 1917–53

The first 'leap forward' in Moscow's metropolitan growth followed the return in 1918 of the administration under Lenin to Moscow as capital of the new Soviet State, together with the introduction of new economic planning functions and the centralization of control which transferred much decision-making and paperwork for farms, factories and towns throughout the country to Moscow. The second 'leap forward' came with Stalin's First and Second Five Year Plans (1928–32, 1933–7). These initiated massive industrialization to replace specialization in consumer textiles by the production of capital goods, mainly machinery. Concentration of new jobs, especially in Moscow, unleashed unprecedented problems of material and energy supply, overcrowded housing, strategic vulnerability, and transport to cope with the growth in freight and journeys to work.

Simultaneously, farm collectivization (1931–3) created social and economic problems in rural areas and shortages of food in urban areas, yet stimulated city-ward population migration. So rapid and problematic was the metropolitan agglomeration that the Third Five Year Plan (1937–41) required the restraint of city growth and the diversion of jobs to other economic regions. The Nazi invasion during the Second World War enforced this. Industries were evacuated to the Urals, whilst the Moscow region suffered heavy loss of life and property, creating problems of reconstruction and labour scarcity during the Fourth Plan (1946–50).

Modernization since 1953

The fundamental problem of the past twenty-five years has been in containing metropolitan growth, whilst vigorously adapting the region to the changing needs and aspirations of post-Stalinist Soviet society. The task is formidable: planned modernization has generated powerful growth processes throughout the Fifth (1951–5) and abortive Sixth (1956–60) Five Year Plans, the Seven Year Plan (1958–65), and the Eighth (1966–70) and Ninth (1971–5) Five Year Plans.

The introduction of automation and mass-production techniques has intensified existing, and created new, regional demand for machine tools and electronic equipment, giving major impetus to industries established before 1941. A changeover from coal to oil, gas, and electricity has generated a demand for chemical and refinery products and the supply of new materials (like plastics) for further manufacture. Policies to raise personal living standards since 1958 have expanded the traditional (textile, shoe, food, furniture) and new (electrical appliance) consumer-goods industries, have developed prefabricated construction industries to cope with an unprecedented housing drive, and have increased tertiary employment in services and amenities. Scientific research and technological development has been stimulated by Soviet space, military, industrial, and health programmes. Integration with Eastern Europe within Comecon has strengthened the economic nodality of Moscow in the socialist bloc, more than offsetting the disadvantages of its great distance from the rapidly developing, resource-rich regions beyond the Urals.

The inertia built into both the structure and the location of activities and infrastructure by earlier planned growth complicated later planning. The planning organization was inadequate to grapple with changing concepts in an ever more complex economy. There was a delayed awareness of the spatial dimensions of urban and regional problems, and there were changes in policy especially in the 1960s, making the solution of the region's problems harder.

Thus in 1970, on the eve of the current Ninth Five Year Plan (1971–5) Soviet geographers identified numerous economic problems still manifest in the city region. Industries consuming large quantities of fuel, power, and metals transported from afar continue to expand. Some consumer-goods and specialized-components industries still do not satisfy the regional demand. Resource use is uneven: while timber resources are fast disappearing owing to over-cutting, local fuel resources are under-utilized. Delayed farm modernization still constrains regional supplies of livestock fodder, dairy and meat products, fruit, and vegetables. The concentration of development in and around Moscow has hindered peripheral areas and small and medium-sized towns, producing sub-regional imbalances between job opportunities and labour supply. Finally, there is a lack of regional policy in the fields of environmental pollution, water supply, and sewage disposal. That these problems needing solutions are identified systematically at all is the hallmark of a planned economy.

4　The Spatial Dimension of Problems

Some problems occur only in certain areas of the Moscow city region: fodder shortages for livestock or the environmental degradation from strip-mining. Others are widespread: the stagnation of small towns, the speed of modernization, labour supply, and transport provision. Broadly, the range and intensity of problems are inversely related to the distance from Moscow: they increase from the periphery towards the core, reaching a peak in the capital itself. The pattern is asymmetrical. Metropolitan problems are evident at greater distances from Moscow in the 'city-rich' zones to the north-west, north-east, east, south-east and south; at lesser distances in the intervening, especially western, 'city-poor' zones. This asymmetry expresses the geography of inter-regional linkages between Moscow and the Soviet economy at large.

The city region in its Soviet context

Many metropolitan regions maintain or increase their national economic role. Not so Moscow. Its relative industrial importance has declined continually since the mid-1930s: from 40 per cent in 1913 to 13 per cent today. Were the region in a slow-growth economy (like Britain's), a protracted decline in jobs, incomes, and urban environmental quality would result. Being in the forefront of an economy which has been experiencing fifty years of rapid economic growth, the relative decline has run parallel with the phenomenal development of the city region because growth is very much faster (up to four times faster) in other, formerly even less developed regions. So great was the scale of development in the 1930s that even a modest eightfold expansion (cf. sixteen to thirty-twofold increase to the east of the Urals and in the Baltic Republics) since 1940 has sustained the Moscow region as the leading Soviet industrial region, marginally ahead of the Ural and Donetsk-Dnieper regions. Pre-eminence stems especially, however, from high value, precision manufactures which reflect leadership in skills, education, science, services, and decision-making centralized in Moscow.

The city region houses one Soviet citizen in six (17 per cent). Its factories produce 25 per cent of the machinery, tools, electrical equipment, railway vehicles, and furniture; 50 per cent of motor vehicles; and over 75 per cent of textile goods and books. Until the Togliatti/Kama river vehicle complex (Volga region) commenced production in 1972, the Moscow region assembled 80 per cent of all Soviet cars, trucks, buses, and trolley-buses. Though its agriculture excels only in flax and potato production (39 and 20 per cent of Soviet output respectively), these also have contributed to industrial pre-eminence: in linen and alcohol manufacture. The region localizes the training and employment of 23 and 27 per cent respectively of all Soviet university graduates and engineers. These percentages are high considering the numbers involved (326 000 students in higher educational establishments in Moscow alone in 1970), the scale of the economy, and the dozens of other important cities.

Moscow the metropolis

The capital is the lynch-pin of the regional economy, being largely responsible for the above localization. With 2.8 per cent of Soviet population, Moscow provides 4.1 million jobs, 3.6 per cent of all (115 million) or 4 per cent of non-agricultural (90 million) jobs, and is the largest Soviet centre (Table 3) of manufacturing, education, research, social services, administration, transport, retailing and tourism. Factories, employing one-third of the labour force, produce 10–75 per cent of Soviet precision goods destined for investment and consumption. Stores conduct 7 per cent of Soviet retail trade, not surprisingly as 18–20 per cent of all rail and air passengers pass through its terminals (600 million in 1972). Annually, the Moskva river port handles 30 million tonnes (7 per cent of Soviet riverborne cargo), the railways 64 million tonnes (2 per cent of the Soviet total).

Moscow really excels, however, in decision-making and scientific research. One in every ten administrators works there, where all important economic, political, and social decisions are made concerning Soviet–foreign relations, as well as those relating to the U.S.S.R., the R.S.F.S.R., and the city itself. Central planning concentrates in State departments and ministries in Moscow all headquarters of production (farming, finance, fishing, forestry, mining, and manufacturing) and services (wholesaling, transport, tourism, education, research, and medical services) which have more than local significance. Decision-making

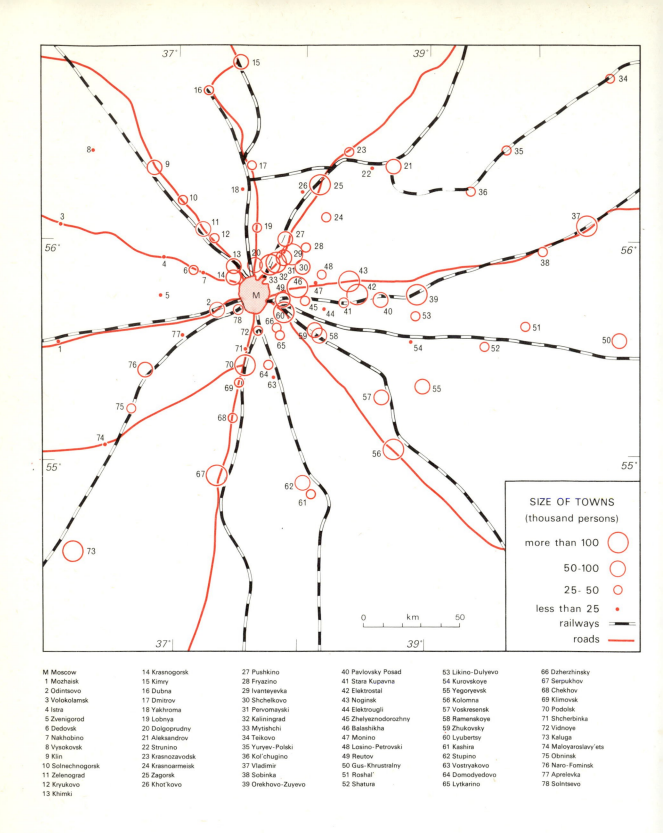

Fig. 7. Urban centres of the Moscow region, 1970

SIZE OF TOWNS
(thousand persons)

more than 100
50-100
25- 50
less than 25
railways
roads

M Moscow	14 Krasnogorsk	27 Pushkino	40 Pavlovsky Posad	53 Likino-Dulyevo	66 Dzherzhinsky
1 Mozhaisk	15 Kimry	28 Fryazino	41 Stara Kupavna	54 Kurovskoye	67 Serpukhov
2 Odintsovo	16 Dubna	29 Ivanteyevka	42 Elektrostal	55 Yegoryevsk	68 Chekhov
3 Volokolamsk	17 Dmitrov	30 Shchelkovo	43 Noginsk	56 Kolomna	69 Klimovsk
4 Istra	18 Yakhroma	31 Pervomayski	44 Elektrougli	57 Voskresensk	70 Podolsk
5 Zvenigorod	19 Lobnya	32 Kaliningrad	45 Zhelyeznodorozhny	58 Ramenskoye	71 Shcherbinka
6 Dedovsk	20 Dolgoprudny	33 Mytishchi	46 Balashikha	59 Zhukovsky	72 Vidnoye
7 Nakhobino	21 Aleksandrov	34 Teikovo	47 Monino	60 Lyubertsy	73 Kaluga
8 Vysokovsk	22 Strunino	35 Yuryev-Polski	48 Losino-Petrovski	61 Kashira	74 Maloyaroslavy'ets
9 Klin	23 Krasnozavodsk	36 Kol'chugino	49 Reutov	62 Stupino	75 Obninsk
10 Solnechnogorsk	24 Krasnoarmeisk	37 Vladimir	50 Gus-Khrustralny	63 Vostryakovo	76 Naro-Fominsk
11 Zelenograd	25 Zagorsk	38 Sobinka	51 Roshal'	64 Domodyedovo	77 Aprelevka
12 Kryukovo	26 Khot'kovo	39 Orekhovo-Zuyevo	52 Shatura	65 Lytkarino	78 Solntsevo
13 Khimki					

TABLE 3
Employment in the city of Moscow, 1970

Economic activity by rank order	Employment (thousands)	Percentage of total city employment (figure for 1960 in brackets)	Percentage of Soviet employment in each activity
Manufacturing	1239	30·2 (36·4)	3·8
Scientific research, development, survey, and design	845	20·6 (15·0)	21·4
Transport and communications	386	9·4 (10·3)	4·0
Construction	270	6·6 (7·6)	4·1
Education	267	6·5 (5·9)	3·0
Retailing and banking	242	5·9 (5·2)	2·9
Housing and communal services	206	5·0 (5·7)	6·4
Health and social services	204	5·0 (4·4)	3·9
Administration	194	4·7 (3·2)	10·1
Catering	111	2·7 (2·3)	3·8
Warehousing	32	0·8 (0·9)	3·1
Other	105	2·6 (3·1)	—

Source: Itogi Vsesoyuznoi Perepisi Naseleniya 1970, Vol. IV; Moskva v Tsifrakh, 1972, p. 65.

depends heavily on organizations which collect, analyse, and supply information for national, regional, urban, and technical planning. Scientific research in Moscow—executed in planning and projecting bureaux, ministries, production and construction enterprises, and the Soviet Academy of Sciences—employs 21 per cent of all Soviet research personnel. Good communications are crucial for the smooth operation of intricate planning and research networks, and the city boasts 15 per cent of the telephones, generates 7 per cent and receives 18 per cent of the inter-city calls in the U.S.S.R. So important is office and social service employment that Moscow, alone among the large Soviet cities, has more than half its labour classified as 'serving' rather than 'working'. Little wonder that women find work opportunities attractive or that 16 per cent of all university graduates and engineers work in the city.

The metropolitan area and its problems
Today 3 million people inhabit the outer metropolitan area (suburban zone: *prigorodnaya zona*) beyond Moscow, mostly in forty-eight towns strung out along eleven radial electrified railways (Fig. 7). Some towns coalesce with the metropolis: Khimki, Dolgoprudny, Mytishchi, Reutov, and Lyubertsy. The majority are spatially distinct, though those to the north-east and south-east tend to form minor conurbations. Functionally, these towns are part of Moscow. Every weekday 500 000 commuters flow from their housing blocks, ride the suburban trains (*elektrichka*) and fill one in every twelve Moscow jobs. At weekends the tide reverses: Muscovites travel out, seeking open countryside, forest, lakes, and summer cottages (*dacha*). All year, intricate linkages are knit between the farms, factories, quarries, laboratories, markets, offices, and construction sites dispersed throughout the metropolitan area.

During the 1960s, the entire metropolitan area absorbed almost the whole population growth of the Central Region (1·9 million), an increase of 22·5 per cent. Employment expanded faster, by 31 per cent (1·75 million jobs), aggravating labour shortages. Trends differ, however, between five distinctive zones, three in Moscow, two outside it (Table 4). Rapid population growth was accompanied by a colossal redistribution of people through migration.

One million new jobs, an increase of 27 per cent, were created between 1959 and 1970, mainly in central and inner Moscow. Since such concentration coincided in time with overspill, it has greatly aggravated the commuter problem. The outward movement of jobs lags behind the massive new residential building in outer Moscow which is designed to alleviate the chronic housing shortages and to raise living standards. As transport improvements also lag, commuting is arduous and time-consuming and depreciates—at least in the short run—the benefits of new and long-awaited apartments.

TABLE 4
Population trends in the Moscow city region, 1959–70

	Area (km²)	Population (thousands) 1959	1970	Percentage change
Moscow city	886	6044	7061	+17
Central area	18	930	420	−55
Inner ring	378	4116	3300	−20
Outer ring	490	998	3341	+335
Outer metropolitan area	7950	2371	3250	+37
Forest Park Belt	1800	931	1200	+29
Outer suburban zone	5950	1440	2050	+42
Rest of Moscow oblast	39 000	2534	2525	−0·3
The periphery	502 000	28 746	29 098	+1

Sources: *Moskva v Tsifrakh*, 1960, 1967, and 1972; *Moskovskaya Oblast za 50 let*, Moscow, 1967.

Central Moscow

Circular in shape, central Moscow is encompassed by the Garden Ring (*Sadovoye Kol'tso*) road and is roughly equal in area to central London (or half the City of Paris). Three-quarters lies on the north (left) bank of the Moskva river; the remainder occupies a meander to the south, opposite the Kremlin.

Located at the very heart of the city, the Kremlin is the great citadel around which were added, in successive epochs before 1700, the three once-walled 'towns' of present-day central Moscow (Figs. 8 and 9). Innermost is *Kitai-gorod* ('China' or 'Fortress' town), sited immediately to the east of the Kremlin. To the north, extending in a crescent between the Yauza and Moskva rivers, is *Bely-gorod* (White town): the line of its outer walls are preserved by the Boulevard Ring (*Bul'varnoye Kol'tso*). Between the Boulevard and Garden Rings lies *Zemlyanoy-gorod* which also embraces the southern area (*Zamoskvorech'ye*: 'beyond the Moscow river'). Zemlyanoy-gorod, literally 'Earth town', derives its name from a 16-km-long earthen rampart (*Zemlyanoy Val*) which encircled it till the nineteenth century when it was cleared for the Garden Ring. Today, a broad functional distinction can be made between the medieval core (the Kremlin, Kitai-gorod, and Bely-gorod) that concentrates the administrative, commercial, and cultural activities, and Zemlyanoy-gorod which is more residential.

The problems of each area derive from its age, functions, morphology and its links with the rest of the city. Common throughout central Moscow, however, are congestion of buildings and traffic and the intermixture of intensive, sometimes incompatible, land-uses. Residential densities are high, ranging from 25 000 persons per km² in Zamoskvorech'ye to 36 000 persons per km² in the north-east. A high concentration of offices and services provides jobs for more than 1 million people. This number has increased substantially since 1959, despite a dramatic two-thirds decrease in residential population. Many specialized and department stores (*Univermag*) handle one-quarter of the city's retail transactions. Three out of every four theatres, concert halls and museums and half the city's hotel beds diversify the central functions. Soviet experts estimate that tourists, day visitors, conference delegates, travellers in transit, and persons 'unaccounted for' exceed one million on an average day.

Traffic congestion is not so obvious, so continuous, or so widespread as in western capitals. Nor is it caused by the 150 000 private cars in the metropolitan area. Rather it results from the very high frequencies of public transport: suburban and metro trains, buses, trolley-buses, trams, official cars, and over 25 000 taxis. These converge on railway termini, metro interchanges, key road junctions and thoroughfares. Each 'peak' hour (07.00–10.00 and 15.00–18.30) 700 buses and trolley-buses serve Marx Prospekt (*Prospekt Marksa*) and 300 metro trains stop at the three-line, three-station interchange Marx Prospekt (formerly *Okhotny Ryad*)–Revolution Square–Sverdlov Square. The Garden Ring is particularly busy. Eight railway termini, seven metro interchanges, and many bus, trolley-bus, and tram termini are located near it. One million commuters traverse Komsomolsk and Kursk Squares daily between suburban railway termini (Kazansky, Leningradsky, Yaroslavsky, Kursky), the metro, and surface transport. Truck traffic is channelled round the Garden Ring to reduce congestion, fumes, and noise in the core: 2000

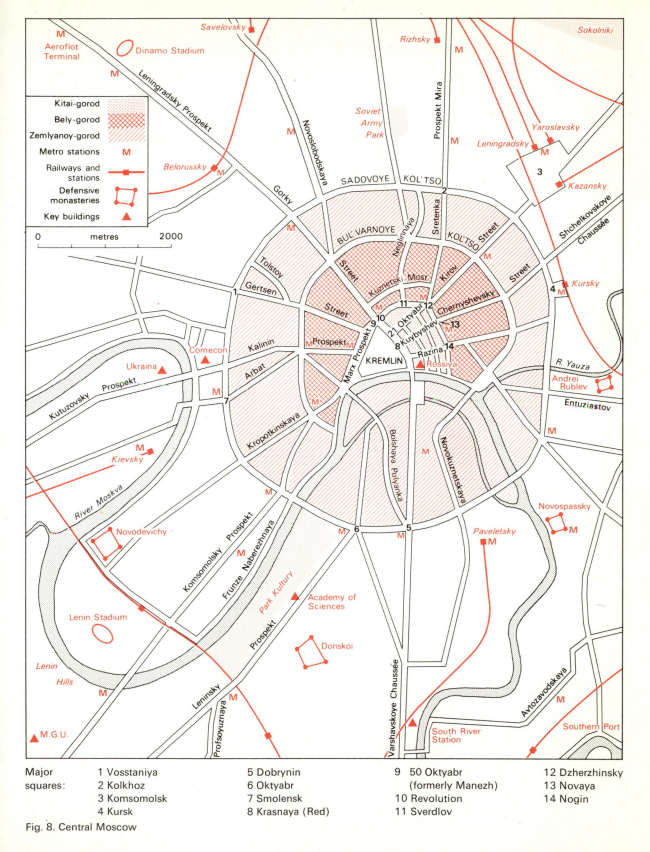

Major squares:

1 Vosstaniya	5 Dobrynin	9 50 Oktyabr (formerly Manezh)	12 Dzherzhinsky
2 Kolkhoz	6 Oktyabr	10 Revolution	13 Novaya
3 Komsomolsk	7 Smolensk	11 Sverdlov	14 Nogin
4 Kursk	8 Krasnaya (Red)		

Fig. 8. Central Moscow

vehicles an hour pass many of its twenty-two intersections *en route* between industrial zones in the south-east, west, and north, and central warehouses.

Narrow streets in Kitai-gorod, Bely-gorod and parts of Zemlyanoy-gorod hinder circulation between the Garden Ring and central squares (Revolution, Sverdlov, Dzherzhinsky, Novaya, and Nogin Squares). Some, like Pushkin or Frunze streets, slope steeply from the Neglinnaya valley (lying below the west Kremlin wall) to the Moskva river terraces. Others, like Arbat (west), Sretenka (north), Novokuznetskaya (south) are flanked by old buildings of mixed retail, warehouse, or artisan use and carry heavy traffic. Congestion in Zamoskvorech'ye, the largest surviving area of pre-Revolutionary building is serious at times as traffic filters through narrow streets *en route* for the central and Garden Ring bridges. Gorky street (*Ulitsa Gorkovo*) is still the only continuously broad highway linking Marx Prospekt with the Sadovoye Kol'tso. Most six- to eight-lane boulevards commence *beyond* the Garden Ring (like Leninsky Prospekt to the south and Prospekt Mira to the north), though new Kalinin Prospekt does extend to the Boulevard Ring (to Arbat Square). Embankment highways flanking the Moskva river provide relief by carrying trucks and cars through central Moscow, but they are discontinuous and are of limited use to commuters.

The interrelations between traffic and land-uses are intimate. Despite great rebuilding since 1917, renewal has not been comprehensive, dealing with problem zones as critical needs required and material supplies allowed. Zones, streets, or buildings renewed in the 1930s, 1950s, and 1960s, mingle with each other and with many preserved from the eighteenth and nineteenth centuries. An architectural and functional mosaic results. Here, old streets and mixed land-uses are preserved especially in south and east Zemlyanoy-gorod and the medieval core. There new arteries and concentrated office or residential complexes are created, notably in central Bely-gorod (Gorky street, east Marx Prospekt), along Kalinin Prospekt, and the Garden Ring—especially the 'wedding-cake' buildings on Smolensk, Vosstaniya, Komsomolsk, and Lermontov Squares, and Kotel'nichesky embankment. Expanding tertiary and quaternary functions have often had to occupy old, cramped buildings ill-suited to their needs, particularly in Zamoskovorech'ye which localizes much research for the Soviet Academy of Sciences. For instance, the Institute of Geography, occupying a three-storey building housing

45 people in 1917 currently employs 500 research staff. Most problematic, however, is the high concentration and intermixture of partially unrelated office, tourist, entertainment, and shopping functions which create hordes of commuters and visitors throughout the day between lower Gorky and Dzherzhinsky streets, Kitai-gorod, and the Kremlin.

Congestion has other important consequences. Sites for new offices and hotels have to be sought beyond the Garden Ring, spreading central area functions. Open space is at a premium, being largely confined to the Kremlin, the central squares, and the Boulevard Ring, though a few small squares (e.g. Repin) and inner courtyards offer much-needed breaks in the built-up area.

The awe-inspiring Kremlin and adjacent Lenin mausoleum in Red Square is a place of compulsive pilgrimage, of magnetic fascination. Opened to the public only in 1956, the Kremlin's tourist capacity is sorely stretched. That opening, however, symbolized the beginning of a more democratic Soviet government, of a greater desire for wider and closer international contacts. These demanded larger, modern facilities inside the Kremlin. The solution, the Congress Palace (*Dvorets Syezdov*) has been cleverly harmonized with the existing complex. As a centre of Soviet political and economic power, history, theatre, and tourism, the Kremlin maintains close ties with the adjacent and somewhat specialized functional zones in central Moscow.

First and foremost are the links with the 'decision-making and information belt'. Its fulcrum lies to the north-east. The political centre is around Novaya (New) and Dzherzhinsky Squares: headquarters of the Soviet Communist Party (or C.P.S.U.) and of the R.S.F.S.R., Moscow, and Youth (or Komsomol) Parties, and the K.G.B. The economic centre is on north Marx Prospekt (Council of Ministers, State Planning Commission or *Gosplan*, Trades Union House) and in north Kitai-gorod between 25th October and Razina streets (ministries of production and commerce occupying premises once owned by private offices, banks, and warehouses). From here the belt extends west along Kalinin Prospekt with its consumer-industry ministries to Comecon headquarters, the Ministries of Foreign Affairs and Overseas Trade (on Smolensk Square), and a galaxy of embassies and trade delegations occupying former aristocratic residences along or near the Garden Ring; and north-east along Kirov street to the Central Statistical Office and the Transport and Communications Ministry near Komsomolsk and Lermontov Squares.

Novosti Press Agency

Information is big business. *Gosplan's* main computer unit processes data on production, services, and welfare from 560 Soviet ministries, research institutes, regional, city, and Comecon bodies for the Five Year Plans

Renewal problems in central Moscow: stately homes, now embassies (centre), and old artisan housing (left) remain as new trade (right) and ministerial offices (back, Kalinin Prospekt) invade the Arbat area

The Kremlin is the hub of an 'educational crescent' extending from Kitai-gorod (Museum of the History and Reconstruction of Moscow, Polytechnic Museum, many professional societies including the Soviet Geographical Society), along Marx Prospekt (Lomonosov University, the huge Lenin Library, Pushkin gallery), the western Boulevard Ring (e.g. the Soviet Chess club on Gogol Boulevard) to Zamoskvorech'ye (Tretyakov gallery, many research institutes). Kremlin theatres (Kremlyevsky Teatr, Dvorets Syezdov) are closely integrated with the 'cultural-entertainment wedge', extending north-west from the Bolshoi Theatre to the Garden Ring between Gertsen and Neglinnaya streets and localizing most theatres, concert halls, and arts centres. Thousands of tourists stay in the hotels of central Bely-gorod and Marx Prospekt (hotels National, Intourist, Moskva, Budapest, Berlin, Armenia, Metropol) or near Moskvoretsky bridge (the Rossiya, the largest in Europe, and the Bucharest). Here also, lying between Gorky and Dzherzhinsky streets and in central Kitai-gorod, is the city's major shopping area with TSUM and Detsky Mir (the 'Central' and 'Children's World' department stores), restaurants (Aragvi, Ararat), and the famous GUM (*Gosudarstvenny Universal'ny Magazin*: state department store) which is capable of serving 20 000 customers an hour.

Long-term solutions to the problems of central Moscow demand a better locational equation between population, jobs, services, and amenities throughout the metropolis. Large areas, especially in the east and Zamoskvorech'ye where old, even wooden, buildings front a confused pattern of lanes, bear the marks of nineteenth-century working-class quarters and require total renewal. Others, notably in the west, where there are many former aristocratic residences with gardens and courtyards, pose a complex problem of preservation versus renewal.

The inner ring

Beyond the Sadovoye Kol'tso, mostly north and east of the Moskva river, spreads a broad, asymmetrical ring as far out as the Circle Railway (*Okruzhnaya Zheleznaya Doroga*), overspilling along radial railways and the river to the east, south-east, west, and north. This is inner Moscow (Fig. 9) today, though such is the speed and scale of metropolitan sprawl that in 1953 it formed the city periphery.

In contrast with central Moscow, the inner ring is dominantly a zone of manual employment and of residential areas for manual workers. Sited here are the vast majority of the city's 1800 factories,

TABLE 5
Manufacturing employment in Moscow, 1913, 1926, 1970

	1913	1926	1970
Electricity generation and supply	*	*	9900
Iron and steel			12 400
Non-ferrous metallurgy			17 350
Machinery, metal-working, and electrical	22 700	39 450	
			688 885
Chemicals and petro-chemicals	12 390	14 340	38 400
Timber-processing and paper	1780	3980	44 600
Building materials and glass	2370	2200	50 000
Textiles and clothing	67 370	64 640	208 150
Food manufacturing	22 710	25 700	68 150
Printing	12 880†	20 765†	40 895
Other	6000	8535	59 470
Total	148 200	179 520	1 239 000

*Figures not available   †Includes also paper manufacture.

Sources: Fabrichno-Zavodskaya Promyshlennost' Goroda Moskvy i Moskovskoi Gubernii, 1917–1927, Moscow 1928; *Moskva v Tsifrakh*, 1970.

engaging a million people (Table 5), 40 per cent of them in large-scale plants with 3000 workers or more. Leading enterprises manufacture vehicles and components (Z.I.L., M.Z.M.A.)*, machinery, electrical and electronic equipment, metals, textiles, chemicals and pharmaceuticals, shoes, foods, cigarettes, books, newspapers, wallpaper, musical instruments, and watches. The inner ring concentrates the massive transport facilities necessary for the functioning of the city's economy. Transport facilities include nine railway passenger termini and 28 intermediate commuter stations; many freight depots (*tovarna*) and huge marshalling yards (*sortirovochnaya*); the Circle Railway that interconnects eleven radial routes for cross-city and transit freight; most railway, metro and

*Soviet factories are all State-owned and planned, hence the non-occurrence of small, duplicated plants, except for those built before 1917. Usually factory names combine in some way the names of (i) famous people (e.g. Lenin, Ordzhonikidze), (ii) what they produce or do, (iii) where they are located, or (iv) revolutionary symbols (e.g. 'October', 'Red Proletariat', 'Sickle and Hammer').

Z.I.L. (*Zavod Imeni Likhacheva*: industrial plant named after Likhachev) is modelled on Ford's Detroit integrated plant, employs 40 000 people, and produces trucks, vans and other heavy freight vehicles. M.Z.M.A. (*Moskovsky Zavod Malolitrazhnikh Avtomobilei*: Moscow Factory for Small-Litre Automobiles) produces the 'Mosvitch' cars and vans.

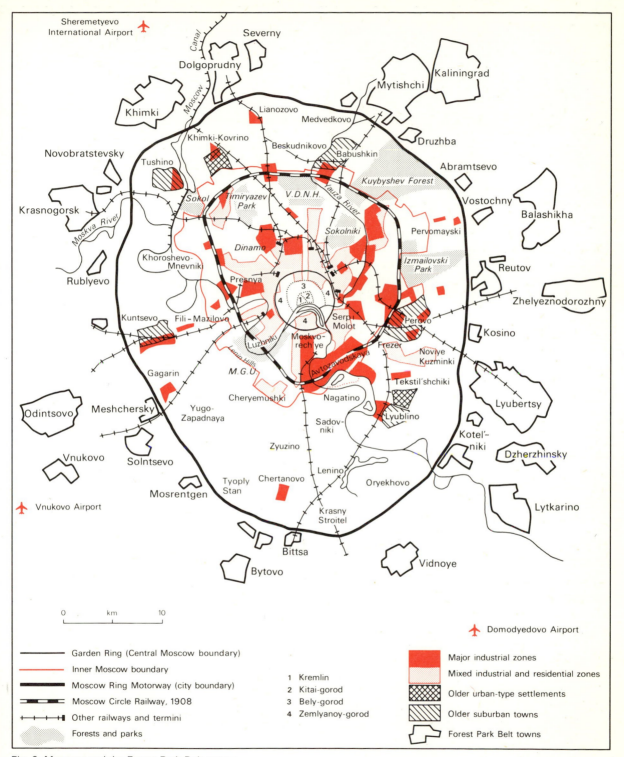

Fig. 9. Moscow and the Forest Park Belt towns

Legend:

— Garden Ring (Central Moscow boundary)
— Inner Moscow boundary
▬ Moscow Ring Motorway (city boundary)
▬ Moscow Circle Railway, 1908
╫ Other railways and termini
░ Forests and parks

1 Kremlin
2 Kitai-gorod
3 Bely-gorod
4 Zemlyanoy-gorod

■ Major industrial zones
▨ Mixed industrial and residential zones
▨ Older urban-type settlements
▨ Older suburban towns
◇ Forest Park Belt towns

Women tramdrivers symbolize policy to reduce labour shortages by full employment of local women

required and generated by this zone since 1940 (Table 6). Rail electrification, which trebled carrying capacities, and the substitution of rail-hauled by piped or transmitted energy, have tempered but not eliminated rail congestion, since much transit freight uses the Circle Railway (to avoid the inadequate bypass lines in Moscow *oblast*), and passenger train frequencies have increased to cope with greater suburban commuter traffic (Table 6).

Road congestion is growing faster. Though the Soviet economy mainly depends on railways, the metropolitan regional economy—manufacturing light, quality products and requiring intensive and intricate spatial linkages over short distances between plants and consumers in Moscow and its urban hinterland—is pre-eminently dependent upon truck transport to an extent unrivalled by other major Soviet cities.

Congestion occurs around major factories, warehouses, and freight depots and on main routes. Strong centripetal forces encourage the construction across inner Moscow of great arterial roads, up to 100 m wide, which converge on the Garden Ring from all directions (Fig. 8). Good transverse roads are virtually lacking, especially across the Moskva river outside the central area, so an undue volume of truck traffic is channelled into the Garden Ring. The Moscow Ring Motorway (*Moskovskaya Kol'tsevaya Avtomobil'naya Doroga*), forming the outer administrative limits of the city, is too far out to relieve inner-zone congestion.

The situation awaits solution. Meanwhile, congestion is further aggravated by the scale and mode of commuter traffic. Trams remain

tram sheds; most garages for buses, trolley-buses and trucks belonging to the city road freight transport organization (*Glavmosavtotrans*); the north, west and south Moskva river ports; and the *Aeroflot* terminal serving the city's three major airports.

Such facilities are the *raison d'être* of inner zone manufacturing and distribution. Industrial expansion, mainly by modernization and automation, has increased enormously the volume of freight

TABLE 6

Volume of traffic originating and terminating in the city of Moscow by mode, 1940 and 1970

	1940		1970	
Freight	million tonnes	percentage	million tonnes	percentage
Railway	27·0	38·1	62·8	20·8
River	5·8	8·2	28·6	9·5
Road	38·0	53·7	210·0	69·7
Total	70·8	100	301·4	100
Passenger	millions	percentage	millions	percentage
Railway (suburban only)	205	7·3	493	9·8
Metro	369	13·0	1642	32·5
Bus	210	7·4	1505	29·8
Trolley-bus	212	7·4	775	15·3
Tram	1848	64·9	639	12·6
Total	2844	100	5054	100

Sources: Moskva v Tsifrakh za Gody Sovyetskoi Vlasti, 1967; Moskva v Tsifrakh, 1972.

Bus congestion in Leninsky Prospekt illustrates commuting problems between rapidly extending, high density, outer housing areas and central and inner Moscow. Note the ground-floor shops and service roads

significant mainly in the inner ring despite a dramatic decline in importance (Table 6). The scale and segregation of both manufacturing plants and the workers' residential areas serving them are such that travel to work by public transport is inevitable, especially in districts like Avtozavod-skaya (Z.I.L., M.Z.M.A.) which developed during the 'gigantomania' phase of the 1930s industrialization. Still more important is stepwise commuting to and from the zone. Thousands of inner-ring residents travel to work in services and administration in central Moscow, whilst the deficit of workers in the inner zone—created both by this efflux and by the huge concentration of manufacturing jobs and transport—is balanced by the great ebb and flow of commuters from new residential areas in outer Moscow and from the galaxy of expanding satellite towns beyond. Most come by train, but since 1956, the massive drive to house people in the outer zone has, in the absence of adequate new metro lines, generated large-scale journeying to work by bus and trolley-bus into and across the inner zone.

Significantly, the inner ring is not homogeneous. Population densities and problems vary between three distinct sub-zones: pre-Revolutionary housing, newer industrial, and non-industrial districts of the Stalin period. Industrial Moscow sprawls along the Circle Railway, its junctions with radial railways, and the Moskva and Yauza rivers (Fig.

9). Outstanding is the huge concentration in the inner south-east and east: the Yauza valley northwards to beyond the Sokolniki Park, around Serp i Molot (Sickle and Hammer), and along the Circle Railway from Shchelkovskoye Chaussée (north) and Perovo/Frezer (south-east) to Varshavskoye Chaussée (west). Other concentrations occur in the west (Presnya/Khoroshevskoye Chaussée area), inner north (Belorussky–Savelovsky—Rizhky railways zone), north-west (Shchukino—Likhobory belt), and north (Rostokino—Yauza zone) i.e. north of the Sokolniki and Exhibition Parks.

1. Older, pre-Revolutionary quarters of working-class housing still encircle central Moscow. Currently, they are scheduled for comprehensive renewal (Fig. 14) because of: overcrowding in dilapidated houses and tenements, often without baths; narrow, often cobbled streets served by trams; cramped, sometimes obnoxious industries and occasional large factories (e.g. Trekhgornaya cotton combine in Presnya) which vie for space with warehouses, a high density of shops (a legacy of the capitalist period), transport depots and housing; and very few open spaces or cultural amenities. These areas bore the brunt of the population explosion in Moscow after 1928: their densities in 1970 still ranged from 12 000 to 23 000 persons per km².

In the 1930s ministries built workers' (analogous to 'company') towns beside big plants like Z.I.L. (above)

2. Problems in the newer industrial areas of the 1930s and 1940s are quite different. Improvement, not renewal, is required. Residential densities are high because wider, tree-lined boulevards and open courtyards are counter-balanced by higher-rising six- or eight-storey housing blocks. But the increased housing supply in outer Moscow is facilitating population reduction, raising *per capita* living space. Many districts were planned on the *mikrorayon* ('micro-district') or neighbourhood, principle: the Profsoyuznaya, Izmailovskaya-Pervomayskaya, Avtozavodskaya, Kutuzovskaya,

and Shcherbakovskaya districts. Symptomatic of Soviet preoccupation with labour is the average provision of school, crêche, and medical services but poor provision of retail services (Table 7). Indeed 'shopping centres' by our definition do not exist in these districts. Retail outlets occupy ground floors of housing blocks on major streets, or kiosks near transport nodes, and supply the bare needs in groceries, medicines, household goods, newspapers, and laundering. Usually one *Univermag*, but few other stores selling consumer durables, are located in each district. Theatres are rare, cinema provision below average, parks and recreation spaces limited. Higher educational facilities are also deficient beyond 'factory-floor' training in skills. For all these services, residents must go to central or older, inner Moscow.

Such an environment could perpetuate social or occupational immobility to an extent considered undesirable by a Soviet society which is bent on maximizing social mobility and preventing the emergence of 'ghettoes'. Though distances to metro stations are greater than in older zones, an increasing number of young people, the first generation born in these *mikrorayons*, travel to study or to work in non-manufacturing jobs elsewhere. This trend is associated with the labour shortage and the problems of manufacturing in the inner ring which, in turn, reflect basic changes in the metropolitan economy. The year 1966 marked the turning point: for the first time in fifty years of Communism the growth of manufacturing employment in Moscow stopped. Indeed, a decrease of 112 000 jobs (0·9 per cent) was recorded between 1967 and 1970, a figure undoubtedly exceeded in the inner ring as new industry developed in outer Moscow. Most plant closures involve small, cramped or obnoxious industries in older industrial areas like the Yauza valley and Luzhniki. Now, larger industries in newer zones are under scrutiny for potential relocation outside

TABLE 7

Some indicators of service and amenity provision by zones of Moscow, 1970
(per thousand population)

	Students in all forms of education	Library books and journals	Hotel beds	Hospital beds	Cinema seats	Trade turnover (1000 rubles)	Population per hectare of open space, parks, and forest
Central area	315	162 000	21	11	23	3875	} 606
Inner ring	260	39 200	2	12	8	1621	
Outer ring	170	8580	4	11	10	891	221

Sources: *Moskva v Tsifrakh za Gody Sovetskoi Vlasti, 1967; Moskva v Tsifrakh 1970, 1972.*

the city. First in line for removal are industries which are beyond modernization, have weak linkages with metropolitan activities, depend mainly on labour from outside Moscow, or give 'the south-east the worst emissions, greatest smoke and the worst health and hygiene environment for the residential population in all the capital'.[*] Already paints, gas, chemicals, furniture, textile, and foundry works have been dismantled, casting doubt also on the future of the 'Serp i Molot' steelworks. The land released by this process poses complex redevelopment problems which can be solved only by comprehensive and regional planning. Usually, production units are removed and replaced by expanding research facilities for similar industries. Surplus land will, in the long-term, offer space at nodal points for the much-needed provision of services and other amenities.

3. The essentially 'non-industrial wedges' and periphery of the inner ring have in the past accommodated the growth in tertiary and quaternary functions outside central Moscow. There are four such wedges. The north-east wedge, by far the largest, centres on north Prospekt Mira and comprises Ostankino, V.D.N.H.[†], Sokolniki, and the huge Kuybyshev *rayon* forest. The north-west includes Leningradsky Prospekt, Timiryazev, and southern Khimki Reservoir. The east contains Izmailovski Park. The south-west straddles Kutuzovsky, Komsomolsky, and northern Leninsky Prospekts and embraces Park Kultury, Luzhniki, and the Lenin hills.

Indistinguishable in their monumental architecture from other areas of 1930–50 vintage, the aesthetic monotony of these districts has gradually mellowed as the trees lining the boulevards grew taller. There ends the similarity with, say, Gorky street or Avtozavodskaya. Functions and environment in these wedges are quite distinct. The dominant features are the 'lungs' of the city: large open spaces, parks, forests, and amenities devoted to recreation, education, and culture. The leading recreation wedges are in the south-west (the huge Lenin Luzhniki stadium and sports complex, Park Kultury, the new circus) and the north-west (bathing, boating, excursions on Khimki reservoir, and the Dinamo complex of swimming pools and soccer, cycling, athletics, and horse-racing stadia). Forests and parks dominate the

[*]Yu. G. Saushkin, *Moskva : Geograficheskaya Kharakteristika*, Moscow, 1964, p. 203.
[†]V.D.N.H. is pronounced *Ve-De-eN-kHa* in Russian. It is the abbreviation for *Vystavka Dostizhenii Narodnovo Khozyaistvo* (Exhibition of the Achievements of the National Economy).

Sokolniki park forms a popular green 'wedge' between the Yauza and inner northern industrial zones

north-east: Sokolniki, Kuybyshev, and Izmailovski. Education and research are concentrated in the northern wedge: the impressive V.D.N.H. and Soviet Academy of Sciences' botanical garden and Timiryazev agricultural park.

Pleasant environments have encouraged planners to develop services and research facilities in all wedges except Izmailovo, which suffers air pollution from the industrial south-east but is no less accessible from central Moscow. Hotels, early localized in the south-west (Ukraina) and recently extended along Leninsky Prospekt, have been grouped to the east and west of V.D.N.H. and along Leningradsky Prospekt (*Aeroflot* Terminal). The 'media' are prominent: radio, television and *Mosfilm* studios (south and south-west), the new Ostankino television centre near V.D.N.H., *Pravda* newspaper headquarters near Dinamo. Research, design, medical and educational institutes concentrate in the south-west, linked functionally with the Soviet Academy of Sciences and Moscow University, and in the north-west (*Gidroproyekt*, the water research institute near Sokol, and thirty other establishments). Decision-making functions overspill the central area into the south-west, along Frunze Naberezhnaya.

Far more service and research personnel live in

Yugo-Zapadnaya (outer Moscow). Note the 5-storey economy flats of 1960, the newer high-rise flats, the *mikrorayon* school (centre) and cinema (under construction), the lack of shops and garages

these 'wedges' than in the industrial zones. Areal social differentiation tends to be sharpened by the attraction to these wedges of many central-area office workers (as in the Peschanaya district near Sokol) and of thousands of foreign embassy staff, trade delegates, and reporters who are segregated in patrolled blocks in select areas of the Kutuzovsky, Leningradsky, and Prospekt Mira wedges. But more manufacturing workers live in such districts by comparison with western cities.

The wedges suffer similar, though less daunting, problems than elsewhere in the inner ring. Retailing, cinema, and educational provisions are better than in industrial areas, but need improvement. The major problem stems from the Soviet predilection for gigantic complexes. The Dinamo, Luzhniki, Park Kultury, and V.D.N.H. complexes seriously aggravate congestion on busy arterial routes and metro stations close to central Moscow.

The outer ring

The third zone, between the Circle Railway and the Ring Motorway, is a belt of massive residential building, undertaken since 1956. Twenty years ago, agricultural land and forests were punctuated by villages, a few 'urban-type settlements' like Khovrino and five older industrial towns: Babushkin, Perovo, Lyublino, Kuntsevo and Tush-

ino. Fewer than a million people lived there. Today almost 4 million do so. Villages have disappeared, the five towns have been absorbed into the metropolis and expanded. Most of the inhabitants, however, occupy apartments built on virgin sites in new districts, each with 150–300 000 people: Khimki-Khovrino, Beskudnikovo/Lianozovo, and Medvedkovo (north); Noviye Kuzminki and Nagatino (south-east); Cheryemushki, Zyuzino, and Chertanovo (south); Yugo-Zapadnaya and Gagarin (south-west); Fili-Mazilovo and Khoroshevo-Mnevniki (west) (Fig. 9).

The five older towns exhibit, on a small scale, the problems of inner industrial Moscow, but they are spared congestion as they lie off major highways. The major problems are in the new districts where the scale and speed of apartment-building has far outstripped the provision of retailing, social services (Table 7), transport, and employment.

Initial problems emerged in planning the residential areas. In the 1950s, the rapid assembly of standardized prefabricated sections offered a solution to appalling housing shortages. Under Khrushchev (1956–64), economy in housing construction was considered necessary while investment supported Soviet industrial expansion, space programmes, and agricultural extension into the virgin semi-arid steppes. Under the Seven Year Plan (1958–65) enormous areas adjacent to the inner ring in the north (Likhobory Verkhniye–Beskudnikovo) and south (Leninsky Prospekt) were uniformly covered with identical five-storey blocks without lifts. So great was the housing drive after 1956 that by 1966 such blocks provided two-fifths of Moscow's entire housing space. This policy (i) created incredibly soulless residential districts; (ii) yielded relatively low-density housing which has proved costly to service with water, gas, electricity, thermal heat, public transport, and refuse collection; (iii) increased average travel times to service points for residents; and (iv) caused a land shortage. This last is important. The Soviet context of vast open spaces is not at all the Moscow regional context. Had rehousing continued on the same pattern, residential areas would now swamp the entire outer ring, overspill the Ring Motorway and engulf satellite towns and open land beyond.

Policies were altered dramatically in 1964. Districts built since then (e.g. Yugo-Zapadnaya, Chertanovo, Nagatino) exploit the architectural advantages of prefabricated building and combine 7- to 10-storey 'wall-type' blocks with 9- to 16-storey towers. The continued high rates of construction have thus created in the outer ring a series of high-density residential 'fortresses'. By 1971, 8- to 16-storey (or higher) buildings provided 39 per cent of all Moscow housing space compared with 20 per cent in 1966. New districts offer more spacious living, but the standards of finish, quality, and modernity of fittings are still sacrificed to speed and economy of construction.

Once Muscovites obtain their new apartments, they face much longer journeys to work. As yet only a minority of people move here from outside Moscow. Two-thirds of outer-ring residents work in inner and central Moscow. For many a 10- to 20-km or 40- to 60-minute journey by bus and metro replaces a former 1- to 10-km or 5- to 30-minute bus, trolley-bus, tram, or metro journey. Express buses are crowded beyond belief, especially those plying, even at 1- to 2-minute intervals, between the metro circle line stations and the outer districts. Pressure is caused by the absence of metro lines to the outer northern, southern, and western districts, the convenient routing of buses and the greater expense of travelling the alternative *elektrichka*. For example, a journey from Chertanovo to the Paveletsky terminus by *elektrichka* costs 40 kopeks, charged according to distance; by bus over the same route the flat rate fare is 5 kopeks. The train takes 22 minutes, the bus 48 minutes. Commuting is complicated further since most new residential development is to the south-west, whereas most

jobs are north and east of the Moskva river. This generates more traffic across central Moscow or from Zyuzino-Chertanovo to the south-eastern industrial district.

Since State policy restricts manufacturing growth in Moscow, job creation in the outer ring is dependent upon relocation of industries, laboratories, research institutes—but not as yet offices—from inner-ring or central-area sites. Such decentralization is a complex, tardy process, so far not guaranteeing that activities will form interrelated complexes or offer that mix of jobs which matches the sex structure and skills of the newly resident population. Efforts are certainly made to do so, by the radial movement of jobs and people to maintain the principle of providing work near residence. Research institutes have been relocated from Zamoskvorech'ye to Yugo-Zapadnaya, industries from Presnya to Khoroshevo-Mnevniki or from Savelovsky to Beskudnikovo. Noticeably, though, the industries located in the outer ring are more 'footloose', more dispersed, and less tied to railways than the industries of inner Moscow.

That retailing (Table 7) lags far behind housing construction in outer Moscow reflects the inexperience and indecision of planners with respect to retail location. In the 1960s, shops continued to be provided under residential blocks, but groups of highly specialized stores were introduced on major thoroughfares. Large stores on middle Leninsky Prospekt selling clothes, cameras, furniture, and toys provide examples. Such 'shopping centres' proved inconvenient to get to from wide catchment areas. Shops were too specialized and too few as well as being 'strung out' over long frontages, widely spaced, and divided by boulevards 100 m wide with few pedestrian crossings or subways. In the latest districts, therefore, 'experimental' groups of shops selling both everyday and durable goods are being introduced at road junctions and around metro stations (e.g. Ryazansky Prospekt). Improvements in retail provision clearly depend on the results of these experiments.

The suburban ring

The 109-km Ring Motorway forms the administrative boundary between Moscow and the suburban ring in Moscow *oblast*. It symbolizes two forces which shape suburban problems: functional subservience to Moscow, and the dominance of 'sector' planning (fostering centralization) over regional planning (fostering decentralization). The Ring Motorway is the outermost, the one 'bypass' route around Moscow linking together all the suburban areas. Rarely are towns on different radial routes interconnected by road or rail independently of the capital: only Kaliningrad is linked with Elektrougli via Shchelkovo, Krasnogorsk with Odintsovo. The motorway's administrative role—to prevent metropolitan sprawl—loses effect against its economic role to stimulate integrated metropolitan and suburban growth. Threatening the suburban ring is the danger that the Ring Motorway could become in the 1980s to the entire metropolitan region what the Circle Railway was to Moscow in the 1930s.

Strong and diversified metropolitan influences intensify competition between land-uses. Forests, traversed by the rivers Moskva, Klyazma, Pakhra, and Yakhroma are in great demand for tourist complexes (especially on the Klyazma and Uchinskoye reservoirs in the northern green belt), as are old villages for *dacha* colonies run by State, trade union, C.P.S.U., and other organizations or owned by individual Muscovites. State farms (like Belaya Dacha) and collectives are required to supply dairy products, fruit, and vegetables from intensively-worked fields and from the largest concentration of glasshouses in the U.S.S.R. Dividing the countryside into rural wedges are rows of towns along radial routes. They house 75 per cent of the suburban population as well as the manufacturing which provides most of the local jobs. Industries were developed after 1928 to exploit the advantage of plentiful land, bringing work to an agriculturally-overpopulated hinterland and satisfying the expanding demand in Moscow for intermediate and finished goods. The products are electro-steel (from Elektrostal), metro trains (Mytishchi), farm machinery (Lyubertsy), sewing machines (Podolsk), cameras and cement works' equipment (Krasnogorsk), and buses (Likino-Dulyevo). Production of machinery, electrical goods, and textiles is very widespread.

Urbanization after 1928 began to exert pressure on land and led in 1935 to the establishment of the *Lesoparkovy Zashchitny Poyas* (Forest Park Protective Belt). Competition for the land has sharpened under the continued, large-scale expansion of Moscow and as a result of the increased efforts to contain the metropolis by diverting more growth into the suburban ring. Symptomatic are the recent demographic trends. The 1959–70 increase of 1·9 million people in the Central Region was shared almost equally between Moscow (53 per cent) and the suburban ring (45 per cent).

The Forest Park, already housing 900 000 people in 1959, had to absorb 30 per cent more (Table 4). This casts serious doubt upon the adequacy of green belt policy. No fewer than twenty-four settlements, ranging in size from a few dozen apartment blocks (*posel'ky gorodskovo tipa*: 'urban-type settlements') to medium-sized towns, lie close to the Ring Motorway within the Forest Park Belt, virtually coalescing with Moscow (Fig. 9). Certain green-belt towns doubled in size (Odintsovo, Dolgoprudny, Reutov, Vidnoye), some by over 50 per cent (like Khimki, Lyubertsy, Kaliningrad or Balashikha). Completely new towns grew from villages or on virgin sites, such as Solntsevo, the 'construction-workers' town. Apparently, the policy to restrict urbanization was successful only in so far as growth was faster in outer suburban towns, yet many of these are sited adjacent to the Forest Park: Lobnya, Pushkino, Fryazino, Podolsk, Dedovsk, and three new towns, Zelenograd (72 600 in 1970), Kryukovo (25 000), and Vostryakovo (18 575). Indeed, urban expansion was faster nearer Moscow irrespective of town size (Table 8), though generally towns with more than 50 000 people grew fastest throughout the city region. Planning did, however, steer the most rapid growth into the north, south, and west 'city-poor' sectors rather than into the highly urbanized east.

Environmental conflicts do not result only from urban expansion. A huge cement and prefabricated-building-sections industry extracts enormous quantities of sand, gravel, stone, and water. Decentralization of industry from Moscow increases land needs and pollution, though care is exercised to confine industrial expansion in the Forest Park to 'clean' machinery and instruments production or to replace obnoxious industries by research (for example, gas-chemicals at Rastorguyevo/Vidnoye). Once the old Moscow-Tushino airport became inadequate to handle increased traffic and larger aircraft, three new airports were built in or very near the Forest Park Belt (Fig. 9).

Growth of industries and services has not eliminated commuting. Nor will it so long as employment expands in Moscow and labour is permitted to move into the suburban ring from outside. Half the able-bodied people of the green belt work in Moscow, a proportion which decreases sharply with distance; yet overall, one in every three suburban workers hold metropolitan jobs. The majority travel by *elektrichka* from within 40 km of central Moscow, though commuters from Noginsk, Balashikha, and small settlements use buses. Many commuter trains commence their journeys 50 to 60 km out (Fig. 10) to handle 'stepwise' commuting from 'end-of-the-line' stations to intermediate industrial towns like Lyubertsy or Podolsk, whence other workers

TABLE 8

Rates of population growth in cities, 1959–70, by city size and distance from Moscow
(1959=100; numbers of cities in brackets)

Distance from central Moscow	City population				
	20 000–50 000	50 000–100 000	100 000–250 000	250 000–500 000	500 000
20–50 km	172 (16)	191 (11)	135 (4)	—	—
50–100 km	122 (8)	132 (4)	116 (4)	—	—
100–200 km	121 (2)	187 (8)	135 (4)	140 (3)	—
200–500 km	118 (37)	120 (10)	139 (9)	136 (3)	126 (2)

Source : Based on *Itogi Vsesoyuznoi Perepisi Naseleniya 1970 goda*, Vol. I.

Fig. 10. Suburban train frequencies in the Moscow area

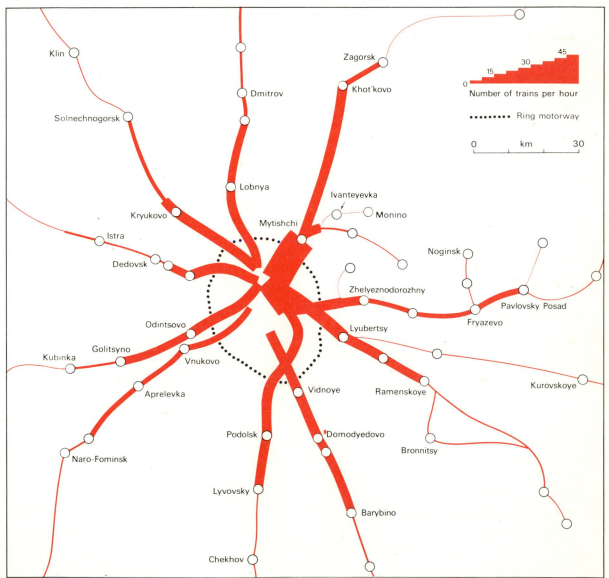

commute to Moscow. Few towns are self-sufficient in jobs and do not send commuters to Moscow.

Decentralizing one job in eight from the capital to convert suburban towns from 'dormitories' to 'self-sufficient' towns would not appear to be beyond Soviet planning capabilities. Yet real difficulties arise. Substantial residential and occupational mobility would be required between Moscow and suburban towns. Administrative, research, and skilled personnel are reluctant to move out of Moscow, fearing deprivation of easy access to the city's huge range and quality of amenities. Office decentralization is restricted by the Soviet need for close central supervision of decision-making and research. The advantages of moving manufacturing may be circumscribed until the construction of good transport 'rings' beyond the suburban zone (combined with the careful relocation of linked industries at key nodes), creates conditions comparable with those currently vested in the intricate production and research linkages within Moscow. Hitherto this constraint has been obviated by directly initiating in suburban locations new industries applying simpler assembly and production techniques, and new plants of established industries serving expanded demand. These industries produce goods for wide regional consumption using components supplied by Moscow factories (e.g. ready-mix concrete trucks using Z.I.L. chassis, motorcycles, lifts, metro trains) or intermediate products sent from other towns of the city region (e.g. finished plastic goods made of P.V.C. material supplied from the Yaroslavl' or Ryazan' oil refineries). Decentralization of employment is also hindered by divided planning responsibilities. This will be examined in the next chapter.

The periphery

The remainder of Moscow *oblast*, the Central Region, and the margins of the city region beyond this, constitute 'the periphery'. Though large in area, diversified in landscapes, resources and functions, it derives unity from the problem of declining population associated with its relative economic disadvantage.

Farms have doubled their output since 1956, mainly as a result of the amalgamation of collective (*kolkhoz*) into enlarged State (*sovkhoz*) farms, and by permitting tighter planning control over, and facilitating greater investment in, agriculture. The State-owned *sovkhoz* is considered to be superior to the *kolkhoz* (in which peasants retain nominal ownership rights) and, under Stalin, *kolkhozy* received little capital. The disbandment of mach-ine tractor stations which formerly supplied farm machinery services, and the sale of machines to *kolkhozy*, has assisted better farm management. Greater areal specialization, exploiting natural advantages more thoroughly, is raising yields. Northern farms—in Vologda, Yaroslavl', Kalinin, Ivanovo, and Ryazan' *oblasts*—have substituted fodder and livestock-rearing (aimed at milk and meat production), poultry and flax (linen manufacture), for oats and rye. Southern farms, from Bryansk through Tula to Tambov, devote more land to wheat, sugar-beet, and pig-rearing. Farms in Moscow *oblast* have turned to intensive vegetable, fruit, and factory-farming. Industrial progress is harder to assess: statistics are not published for *oblasts* and economic regions of the long-term performance of aggregate or growth industry. Available data show, however, a doubling of aggregate industrial output between 1965 and 1970, and a three- to fivefold expansion of long-established textile, food, and timber industries since 1940.

By Soviet standards such growth is below average, resulting in slower improvements in living standards than elsewhere, so encouraging young people, who are more conscious of this issue, to migrate. The situation results from several interrelated factors. Soviet policy since 1932 has diverted development progressively into other regions. The resultant 'slow' growth within the region, however, has been constantly channelled into Moscow and the suburban ring, creating there a high volume of new jobs. Between 1951 and 1970 Moscow (excluding the suburban ring) absorbed 32 per cent of all capital investment in the Central Region, 55 per cent per capita above the regional average. Agriculture is still a major activity outside the larger *oblast* administrative cities but remains relatively depressed, operating as a 'push-factor' from rural areas. Investment in modernization has been inadequate as capital flowed mainly into better and virgin farmlands in other economic regions. Rural development has been hampered by poor provision of roads. Even outer areas of Moscow *oblast* (like Taldom and Zaraisk) lacked hard-surface roads in 1950, and the network everywhere is totally inadequate. Diffusion of basic amenities like piped water, electricity, and medical care has been tardy, especially on *kolkhozy* which still work half the farmland of the city region. And incomes are lower anyway than in urban industry.

Soviet policies have operated unintentionally also to restrict the growth of employment in the towns of the periphery, thereby stunting their ability to arrest population losses to Moscow (and

Leningrad). Most of the 200 small and medium-sized towns (under 50 000 population) have not been chosen for the development of large-scale or growth industries; they must depend upon small, locally-financed extractive, processing, and building activities. This results not from locational disadvantages as much as from poor bargaining power in the planning process *vis-à-vis* the larger of the *oblast* centres for attracting investment in major manufacturing plants and infrastructure. Moreover, the provision of basic social and retail services on *kolkhozy* and *sovkhozy*, and the limits on urban retailing, effectively deprive many towns of central-place functions, and hence jobs, except again the cities which localize *oblast* administration and State-purchasing of farm produce. These policies create in the periphery a situation analogous to Myrdal's model of 'cumulative causation': smaller towns stagnate while growth is localized in a few centres. Since rural areas of the west and south of the city region are among the most densely populated in the European U.S.S.R., many smaller towns are centres of areas which offer the only labour surpluses in the R.S.F.S.R. Remedial action to soak up such surpluses through industrial dispersion began only in the current 1971–5 Plan.

Not surprisingly, therefore, urban growth rates more than 100 km from Moscow are generally lower in the 67 towns with under 100 000 population and higher in the twenty-one largest cities, including all fifteen *oblast*-administrative centres. Larger northern cities (Kalinin, Vologda, Yaroslavl', Kostroma, Ivanovo, Gorky) expanded more 'slowly', by 25–32 per cent between 1959 and 1970, than southern cities (Smolensk, Bryansk, Kaluga, Orel, Lipetsk, Ryazan', Vladimir) which grew by 43–85 per cent. Tula (32 per cent) and Novomoskovsk (25 per cent), alone in the south, experienced slower growth. These variations express the longer-term abilities of major provincial cities to counteract the metropolitan influence. They reflect also the greater rural population densities and potential labour supplies in the south, together with the effects of earlier urbanization and population attraction from both Leningrad and Moscow in the north.

The nature of the urban industrial structure is relevant also. Ivanovo, Yaroslavl', Kalinin, and Kostroma concentrate the cotton, woollen, and linen textile industries, or supply machinery to activities which have low investment priority. The expense of extracting poor resources (cf. Donbass, Kazakhstan, Kuzbass) has restricted coal and steel

expansion in the Tula basin. But diversification into engineering and chemicals has speeded up industrial growth. Southern and eastern towns occupy superb nodal locations between markets in the city region and material and energy supplies from other regions. This factor induced planners, for example, to develop oil refining in Yaroslavl' and Ryazan', and steel in Lipetsk (latterly using Kursk ore). Equally significant is their nodality between component supplies from the metropolitan core and wider Soviet markets. The development of motor vehicle assembly in Gorky (Volga cars, G.A.Z. vehicles) began this trend in the 1930s. It gained momentum after 1950 with the dispersion among leading towns of a wide range of specialized engineering industries, for example, transport equipment (Vladimir, Kalinin, Bryansk), calculators, electrical equipment and appliances (Ryazan', Smolensk, Orel). Closer ties with Eastern Europe through Comecon stimulates more rapid development in western cities like Smolensk. Yet no city in the periphery has experienced the massive structural shift from slow growth consumer-goods to rapid-growth capital-goods and science-based industries that has Moscow.

Other towns of the periphery which are expanding rapidly are of four types. (i) Cherepovets on the northern margin is a new town supporting a large steel industry on a virgin site. It will soon be joined by another on the southern margins in the Kursk 'magnetic anomaly'. (ii) Some towns receive the industrial growth decentralized from major regional centres: Dzherzhinsk (near Gorky), Teikovo (Ivanovo), Rybnoye (Ryazan') and Lukhovitsky (Kolomna, Moscow *oblast*). (iii) Towns lying between the Moscow suburban ring and *oblast* centres or at junctions between radial and ring railways offer labour supply and nodality advantages for industry and research. Examples are Obninsk (in Kaluga *oblast*), Ryazhsk (Ryazan' *oblast*), Yefremov (Tula *oblast*), Safonovo (Smolensk *oblast*) and, most notably, Klin, Stupino, Volokolamsk, and Dubna in outer Moscow *oblast*. Such centres are beginning to benefit from the increased scale of decentralization from Moscow. The siting of the nuclear research centre in Dubna at the confluence of the Moscow canal, Ivankovskoye reservoir, and Volga river, 120 km north of Moscow, is the best example. (iv) A few centres possess rapidly expanding industries based on valuable local resources, such as Voskresensk (Moscow *oblast*) with its chemical industries processing local phosphates.

5 Planning and the Growth of Moscow

The growth of Moscow

Twelve times more people lived in Moscow in 1970 than in 1871 (Table 9). Since the Revolution, the city has witnessed a fivefold expansion in metropolitan population and area, a hundredfold increase in manufacturing output, and growth of the order of eight- to twentyfold in employment, labour productivity, and the supply of housing, social services, and entertainment. Different growth periods are clear. Population quadrupled in the era of railway building, commencing with the Petersburg line (1851) and culminating with the Circle Railway (1908) and the associated capitalist industrialization. War, revolution, and readjustment slowed growth greatly between 1912 and 1926. Massive industrialization and urban reconstruction trebled employment during the first two Soviet Five Year Plans, from 700 000 jobs in 1928 to 2·2 million in 1938, creating an unprecedented population expansion of 2·1 million (2·5 million including the five outer Moscow towns), or almost 200 000 per annum. This phenomenal rate dropped dramatically between 1939 and 1959. The German occupation of the western U.S.S.R. precipitated industrial movement from Moscow, reducing the number of jobs to 1·7 million in 1945, but post-War reconstruction, modernization, and a variable application of planning controls during the Stalin–Malenkov–Khrushchev transition periods ensured almost equal scales of growth in population (by 1·5 million) and employment (by 1·3 million) up to 1959. This trend continued with the annual addition of 100 000 inhabitants *and* jobs in the 1960s.

The expansion of employment has greatly increased activity rates among Muscovites, eliminating under-employment by 1932 and 'housewives', who form only 3·5 per cent of the able-bodied population of working age, by 1970.[*] Commuting and commuter distances have increased, too, partly because the area administered by the Moscow Soviet (*Mossoviet*), the City Council, has been extended periodically (Table 9). Population growth outstripped territorial expansion between 1917 and 1959, raising density from 8130 to 14 175 persons per km². In 1961 the

[*] G. B. Polyak & E. V. Sofronova, *General'ny Plan i Byudzhet Moskvy*, Moscow, 1973, p. 16. See also 'Fall in births threatens Soviet economy', *The Times*, 24 June 1975.

TABLE 9
The growth of the city of Moscow, 1701–1975

Year	Area (km²)	Population (thousands)
1701	21	200
1725	21	175
1811	50	271
1835	71	336
1871	90	602
1897	80	1039
1912	177	1618
1917	228	1854
1926	228	2026
1939	294	4183 (4542)*
1959	356	5046 (6044)*
1970	886	7061
1975	886	7450

*Figures given in the column refer to the population living within the administrative boundaries of Moscow at the time of the census; those in brackets refer to the population living in the present area of the city.

Supreme Soviet of the R.S.F.S.R. decreed the great extension of metropolitan territory to the Ring Motorway to cope with the massive housing programme in outer Moscow. Overall density was still only 8465 persons per km² in 1975.

The planning framework

Such boundary alteration is based on the Soviet conviction that planned development must be unified within the control of one administrative authority. Though laudable, this principle is not applied rigorously in practice. Several suburban 'urban-type settlements' were, before reorganization in 1961, administered by *Mossoviet* and others still are. At present 'city territory beyond the Ring Motorway' includes the four airports, Zelenograd new town (35 km north-west of the Kremlin), six 'urban-type settlements', and two tourist complexes on Klyazma reservoir. This creates 'islands of metropolitan administrative overspill' within Moscow *oblast* which, for its part, is responsible for planning the surroundings, the Forest Park Belt, agriculture, existing industry, and new economic development not relocated as overspill from Moscow. Herein lies a source of conflict between the interests of the city and the regional hinterland, which is sharpened because, like their Western counterparts, these local administrative bodies rely on getting revenue for social infrastructure from the economic activities located on their territory. Whilst, therefore, *Mossoviet* requires land in the suburban ring for housing its workers, it has few incentives to decentralize economic activities into Moscow *oblast*. Similarly, the *oblast* administration has little incentive to develop production and research activities in the settlements administered by the city council. Imbalances between labour supply, jobs, services, and infrastructure thus continue.

To eliminate them requires effective regional planning. Contrary to expectations, no strong bodies have existed to co-ordinate regional policy, except between 1957 and 1964, when Khrushchev initiated the decentralized 'regional' interlude in the long history of Soviet centralized planning. Some 105 (47 after 1962) *sovnarkhozy* (*Soviet Narodnovo Khozyaystva*) or 'economic administrative regions' replaced ministerial control from Moscow, though their role applied to industry and construction only. Agricultural management was devolved to 382 regional bodies, mainly on district or *rayon* scale. Most *sovnarkhozy* comprised one (after 1962 two) *oblasts*, but 'city-regional' *sovnarkhozy* composed of three *oblasts* were formed for Leningrad and Kiev. No comparable organization was created in the Moscow city region which remained divided between Moscow city, Moscow *oblast*, and 16 other *sovnarkhozy*. The very rigid demarcation between them strongly impeded regional planning. The major economic regions—which have fluctuated in size and number (21 from 1921 to 1939, 15 from 1940 to 1960, 17 from 1961 to 1964, 19 currently) and hence lack some stability—possess little regional administrative power.

Paradoxically, great emphasis has been placed, since Lenin's time, on regional issues in locational planning. Yet such concern is translated into practice through centralized 'sector' planning. For several reasons this does not yield regional planning. Central planning aims primarily at Soviet, secondarily at regional, development. The locational principles guiding economic decisions are vague and often conflict, requiring planners within the policy directives of the C.P.S.U. to balance regional specialization against self-sufficiency, resource-orientation against market-orientation, developed and Russian regions against less developed or minority regions, and economic against strategic considerations. Much Soviet research analyses 'territorial-production complexes' which are meant to be highly integrated regional economic organisms. These tend to be idealized geographic interpretations of *ex post facto* Soviet reality, rather than actual tools of regional development policy. Such 'complexes' have evolved mainly in the new regions with simpler economies to the east of the Volga, and are the product of sector planning by industrial ministries. They have been more difficult to introduce into the already developed and intricate Moscow city-regional economy.

Most important, there have been until recently no groups of personnel or decision-making units within *Gosplan* influential enough to make up centrally for the absence of strong regional planning bodies in the country in countering 'sector' interests. Soviet planning is highly centralized but not necessarily comprehensive or co-ordinated. For long it has been dominated by ministries, each of which is responsible for an economic 'sector' such as electricity, oil, steel, machinery, textiles, transport, construction, agriculture, education, or finance. *Gosplan* co-ordinates all-Union and regional balances of inputs (capital, labour, materials, transport) and outputs, but strict control is exercised only over basic capital goods, construction, and transport. The financing of agriculture, housing, and services is more decentralized, to the *oblasts* and cities, but these also vie with each other in bargaining for centralized investment. Thus ministries or their equivalent State directorates dominate the decisions made vertically, often in their own interests, because regional, *oblast*, or city horizontal planning (which tries to integrate the new projects, closures, or expansions proposed by various ministries) is weak. For example, *Mossoviet* may find it hard to persuade the Ferrous Metallurgy Ministry that the 'Serp i Molot' steelworks should be closed in the interests of metropolitan planning until the ministry itself is convinced that the steelworks is no longer viable economically within the Soviet steel industry.

Ministries and State directorates have long sought investment and operational efficiency in using necessarily scarce resources, even before the economic reforms of 1964. Thus, despite the repeated official policy statements aimed at restricting growth, they justify expansion in the Moscow metropolitan area (including central Moscow) and, to a lesser extent, the *oblast* administrative centres, on the grounds of internal and external economies of scale and modernization. This explains the continued imbalances characteristic of the city region's economy as a whole. If expansion demands migrant labour, then a ministry, industrial enterprise (the larger ones are often powerful bargaining forces, though they are often given limited labour quotas), or the

Symptomatic of co-ordination problems in executing plans is this office block near Park Kultury: it stood unfinished for 16 months in 1971–2. Regular street cleansing is a huge consumer of water

Academy of Sciences, will persuade the Ministry of Labour to grant permission (by way of a stamp, like a visa, in the citizens' internal passports) for the necessary personnel to move into Moscow. It appears that there has been even less control of movement into the suburban ring. Such officially sponsored movement is all the greater because permanent workers bring their families. The metropolitan population is further swollen through marriage, seen in the annual 'scramble' for Muscovite husbands or wives by final-year students of M.G.U. who are from other regions yet wish to remain in Moscow. Similarly, the Ministry of Transport has little incentive to encourage reduced commuting on Soviet Railways in the metropolitan area since traffic intensity and widespread shift working ensure 'flattened peaks', efficient use of equipment, and good revenue generation throughout the 24-hour day.

Likewise, *Mossoviet*, and even more the councils in cities like Yaroslavl' or Mytishchi, face enormous difficulties in persuading a multitude of ministries concerned with housing, education, health, trade, transport, electricity, gas, or water—not forgetting the powerful large employers of labour like large industrial plants—to make plans which enable the city to balance demand and supply in new residential areas on either a city-wide or *mikrorayon* basis. Though this situation is general, Moscow has distinct advantages over other towns. As the administrator

of the U.S.S.R.'s 'window on the world', *Mossoviet* commands a respect and bargaining position unmatched by any other council. It has strengthened its position, furthermore, by a long tradition in urban planning, largely monopolizing the limited talents in a field of planning neglected by Soviet governments until the 1960s. Many other towns, including *oblast* administrative centres, have lacked trained urban planners and architects and, hence, the plan guidelines that would facilitate city council control over urban land-uses. *Oblast* control over non-agricultural rural land-uses is often even weaker. This is why the urban threat to the Forest Park is serious. Hitherto suburban town growth has been 'unplanned' in many senses, residential and industrial areas being added—as resources permitted or central decisions demanded—to urban nuclei which sprang up in the capitalist era. Few attempts have been made to create 'dormitory' (e.g. Khimki) or 'self-contained' new satellite towns (e.g. Elektrostal, Zelenograd). Latterly, in the absence of regional controls, councils in several groups of adjacent suburban towns (e.g. Balashikha, Reutov and Zheleznodorozhny) have initiated joint schemes for managing water and land and for protecting environment. Nevertheless, it is in Moscow with its unfinished buildings and problems of traffic, commuters, urban renewal, services, and infrastructure that scale and functional complexity expose planning inadequacies most starkly.

6 Planning Solutions in the Moscow City Region

The first act of the new revolutionary *Mossoviet* in 1917 was to redistribute the city's housing more equitably among the population. Between 1917 and 1920, half a million working people were resettled from older quarters in the inner ring into housing which formerly belonged to middle and upper classes within the Sadovoye Kol'tso. This improved living conditions for only a very short period. The inner ring and central area soon overflowed with new waves of migrants from the countryside. By 1931, when the formulation of the Second Five Year Plan was under way, and Moscow was still on the threshold of massive industrialization, the C.P.S.U. Central Committee, considering the situation to be very serious, decreed that a long-term plan be drawn up to control metropolitan development.

The Moscow plan of 1935

The plan, approved by the C.P.S.U. and Supreme Soviet in 1935 as 'the general Moscow plan' was the world's first comprehensive long-term (twenty-five-year) metropolitan plan, a model for other Soviet cities, and the first to introduce the notion of containing city growth. Basically the plan prohibited new industrial plant construction and restricted expansion to existing activities, primarily to reduce population increase. Whereas the number of inhabitants had doubled between 1917 and 1935 (to 3·66 million), the plan allowed for modest growth to 5 million by 1960. Living and working conditions were to be improved by the generous provision of new apartment housing and open spaces within a city area greatly extended from 285 km² to 600 km², mainly to the southwest, so permitting slum clearance in older areas for the construction of new ring/radial transport arteries (Fig.11). The Forest Park Protective Belt was established to contain sprawl.

The realization of the plan has been only partial. The Second World War and the need for reconstruction from 1945 to 1950 sterilized a decade of potential progress. The execution of the plan also suffered from the monumental nature of its ideas and from inefficient building design (viz. the six 'wedding-cake' skyscrapers) and use of investment. Internal trends also overtook it: policy changes altered priorities after Stalin's death, and new urban planning ideas and prefabricated construction techniques were introduced.

What *did* the plan achieve? Feverish urban renewal was undertaken in central Moscow between 1931 and 1941, using C.P.S.U. guidelines in advance of the final draft of the plan. Slum clearance made way for the central and other squares, widened radial and ring roads (Gorky street, Prospekt Mira, Sadovoye Kol'tso), and created embankment roads, five bridges across the Moskva river, and associated housing, offices and hotels. The first 40 km of metro routes were tunnelled by 1945, forming an X to link central Moscow with parks (the Park Kultury–Sokolniki line, opened 1935) and new industrial and residential quarters (the Avtozavodskaya-Sokol and Izmailovskaya–Arbat lines). Reservoirs (including Khimki), built in the green belt for water supply and recreation, formed part of the Moscow canal project. Opened in 1937 this permitted barge traffic between Moscow and the upper Volga. Despite continued housing shortages, one-third of the metropolitan housing in 1941 was under a decade old.

Following the death of Stalin, the emphasis in Moscow city planning shifted somewhat, for social and political reasons, from transport and infrastructure to greater housing construction. To offset the huge housing deficit, the old central and

Fig. 11. The 1935 city plan: proposed street pattern

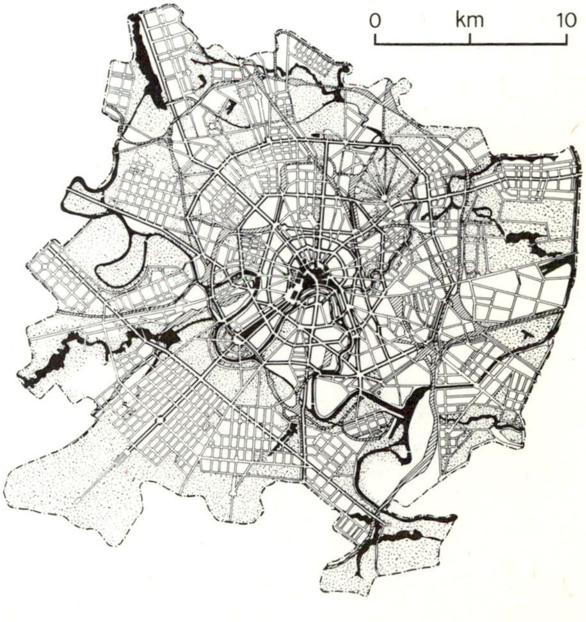

The 'wedding-cake' Ukraina hotel and Vosstaniya flats (left) identify building in Stalin's era. Kutuzovsky Prospekt leads to the Comecon building (middle) and Kalinin Prospekt centre (right), heralding the future central city

inner quarters—though substandard—had to be retained, whilst new residential development spread in the 1950s on to virgin land to the south-west (Yugo-Zapadnaya, Cheryemushki), north-west (Peschanaya), west (Fili-Mazilovo, Khoroshevo-Mnevniki), and east (Izmailovo). The actual location, size, shape, and layout of these housing areas differed from the original 1935 plan, largely through the introduction of the *mikro-rayon*. These were housing districts self-sufficient in social and economic services, incorporating industrialized building techniques and constraints on transport movement.

Indeed, the priority for housing demanded important deviations from the 1935 proposals regarding traffic planning. Only those broad radial roads beyond the Sadovoye Kol'tso were built which would minimize the need for housing demolition in inner Moscow. The south-west radial (proposed in 1935 to pass through the sites of the current Lenin stadium and M.G.U.) and the two ring roads through inner Moscow were shelved. Instead, the Ministry of Transport gave priority to the extension of the metro system to V.D.N.H. and the new residential areas (University, Cheryemushki, Fili, Pervomayskaya), and the central interconnecting *Kol'tsevaya Liniya* (Circle Line), completed 1950–4. Work went ahead on the Ring Motorway to form an 'inter-mediate ring' between the metropolis and the expanding suburban industrial towns which, hitherto, had been poorly served by roads, and to channel some of the increasing volume of truck traffic (especially trucks carrying prefabricated building sections) away from central Moscow.

The 1959 census, counting 5 046 000 inhabitants in Moscow, superficially indicates successful fulfilment of the original 1935 plan in containing metropolitan growth. The census, of course, refers only to the administrative city, then 356 km² which excluded over 500 000 people living in adjacent but separate towns (Kuntsevo, Perovo, partly Tushino and Lyublino) and several 'urban-type settlements' (such as Tekstil'shchiki). Undoubtedly, the plan had assisted *Mossoviet* to exercise control over new industry and population. But the true measure of the success or otherwise of control, was the doubling between 1939 and 1959 of urban development in the zone between the pre-1959 city boundaries and outer limits of the Forest Park. With new industries sprouting up after 1932 in established towns such as Kuntsevo, Lyublino, Lyubertsy, or Mytishchi and creating new towns such as Khimki, Dolgoprudny, Kaliningrad, Balashikha, Zhukovsky, and Krasnogorsk, it is not surprising that by 1950 officials were calling for measures to prevent new industrial construction in the Forest Park Belt.

The 1960s: preparations for a new plan

After 1956, five-storey housing blocks sprawled over the remaining *Mossoviet* administrative area, consuming rapidly the land which the 1935 plan had designated as parkland (on the Lenin hills, for example), threatening coalescence with suburban towns and requiring the construction of new 'urban-type settlements' beyond. Thus in 1960 the Soviet Council of Ministers commissioned Moscow city and *oblast* planning authorities, related research institutes (planning, economics, housing, trade, transport), and development organizations (like *Glavmosstroi*, controlling construction) to devise a 'technical and economic blueprint' for a new general plan. In response to this initiative, the R.S.F.S.R. Supreme Soviet decreed the extension of metropolitan territory to the Ring Motorway in 1961 to embrace an area 275 km² (46 per cent) greater than that defined by the 1935 plan. The Forest Park Belt was simultaneously enlarged and more rigorously defined, suggesting that earlier boundary imprecision had facilitated the uncontrolled urban intrusions into the green belt.

Resource allocations for housing, infrastructure, science, and services under the Seven Year Plan (1958–65), increased under the Eighth Five Year Plan (1966–70) and by *Mossoviet* budgets, shaped the speed and scale of urban change in the 1960s. Within that framework, planning guidelines were derived from the concepts being elaborated simultaneously in the technical and economic blueprint. Completed in 1965, the blueprint permitted the formulation of the new general plan. This reached final-draft stage in 1970.

Unquestionably, the 'struggle for housing' dominated the 1960s. Whole residential districts mushroomed in outer Moscow on a scale and with a speed unprecedented in history. Between 1958 and 1970 some 6 191 000 Muscovites (88 per cent of the 1970 population) moved into larger flats, no fewer than 4 922 000 occupying new apartments. The remainder (1 269 000) were resettled from older quarters in better apartments, built in the inner ring after 1931 (as along Kutuzovsky Prospekt) and vacated by larger families moving to outer Moscow. Urban renewal of former slum areas began, sometimes for housing redevelopment but mainly for service uses (Rossiya hotel, Kalinin Prospekt). Thermal-heating stations, located in the new residential areas on the *mikrorayon* principle, now supply central heating to four-fifths of all Moscow's buildings. Extended and new metro lines offer access to central and inner areas from certain outer southern (Yugo-Zapadnaya, Cheryemushki, Nagatino, Zyuzino,

Noviye Kuzminki) and northern (Khimki-Khovrino) districts, whilst a new central cross link (Prospekt Mira–Oktyabr'skaya) provides direct north–south transit from V.D.N.H. to Cheryemushki. Improvements in surface transport are speeding traffic flows and reducing hazards: two-level interchanges between the Sadovoye Kol'tso and the major radial routes, the Avtozavodskaya and Krasnopresnenskaya bridges over the Moskva river to the east and west of the Garden Ring, and numerous pedestrian subways.

Massive development in advance of the new plan clearly involved risks in making decisions with such large-scale and long-lasting effects. Yet it also permitted a new city-planning flexibility that was entirely appropriate in a less rigid Soviet economic and social environment. The flexibility encouraged, and the scale permitted, Moscow organizations to introduce many urban planning 'experiments' involving design, character, size, function, and servicing. These have proved of great value in finalizing the new plan. The experiments are wide-ranging, concerning new residential *mikrorayons* (Yugo-Zapadnaya 'Eskperimental'ny Kvartal', Noviye Cheryemushki, Chertanovo), but also new retail centres (Vernadskovo and Ryazansky Prospekts), major urban service centres (Kalinin Prospekt) and traffic movement (interchanges on the Ring Motorway, at Gagarin Square on Leninsky Prospekt, or near Savelovsky rail terminus). A major factor assisting the experimentation is the growth of 'co-operative', as distinct from 'State-owned', housing, in which would-be residents can invest their savings and become 'co-owners' with the State in return for 'above-norm' per capita living area, design, and finish. *Mossoviet* has encouraged this trend since 1961 to alleviate pressure on city budgets, to provide higher standards of accommodation, and to create 'living laboratories' for planners. Some 12 per cent of all the housing built between 1961 and 1970 in Moscow was 'co-operative' housing. What experiments have so far failed to do is to indicate how the future plan will provide for the growth in car ownership in existing and new residential areas and service centres.

Moscow 2000: the general plan of 1971

The second general plan for Moscow was approved by the Central Committee of the C.P.S.U. and by the Soviet Council of Ministers in June 1971. Though spanning a period of 25 to 30 years, it is back-dated to 1961, and makes longer-term projections towards the year 2000. The plan is surely destined to become a landmark in Soviet planning history. For the plan makes radical departures from the 1935 plan in city–region relationships, transport, and the provision of services. In so doing it reflects a maturity of city planning based on long experience.

The plan's aims are several. Moscow city and *oblast* are to be planned as one unit to contain and to redistribute metropolitan growth on a regional scale. The metropolis and its satellite towns are to develop in a star-shaped pattern with broad green 'wedges' penetrating deeply towards central Moscow to provide maximum access to open space. Major new service centres, constructed in outer Moscow, will transform the city from its current 'monocentric' to a future 'polycentric' form. Old zones in inner Moscow will be comprehensively renewed, care being exercised to preserve objects of historic, cultural, artistic, or recreational value. Regional and urban transport is to be modernized by means of a new motorway system. The elimination of air and water pollution will improve the environment. Greater efforts will be made to coordinate sector and regional economic planning with physical (town and country) planning.

The regional framework

Integration of Moscow city and *oblast* within the 1971 general plan yields a veritable metropolitan-centred regional plan. A unified regional approach has emerged from *Gosplan* initiatives to strengthen the spatial dimensions of Soviet planning by establishing a special regional research and advisory unit within its organization, S.O.P.S. (*Soviet Organizatsii Proizvoditel'nykh Sil*: the Council for the Organization of Productive Forces).

The regional economic guideline is to be a slow expansion rate in jobs. Strict control over immigration by the passport system is extended from the metropolis to the entire Moscow *oblast*. Soviet economic plans will ensure substantial capital transfers from the region to sustain industrialization in resource-rich regions in Siberia, the Far East, Kazakhstan, and Central Asia. Significant structural shifts in the regional economy will entail a relative decline in manufacturing in favour of the long-neglected service sector. Industrial expansion, confined to precision industries (engineering and electronics) and consumer goods, will be offset by the removal of outdated plants and industries lacking intimate regional linkages, and by a reduction in industries consuming large quantities of raw materials, energy, and water (e.g. metallurgy and chemicals). Similarly, growth in research and related activities

Fig. 12. The 1971 plan: Moscow *oblast* planning areas

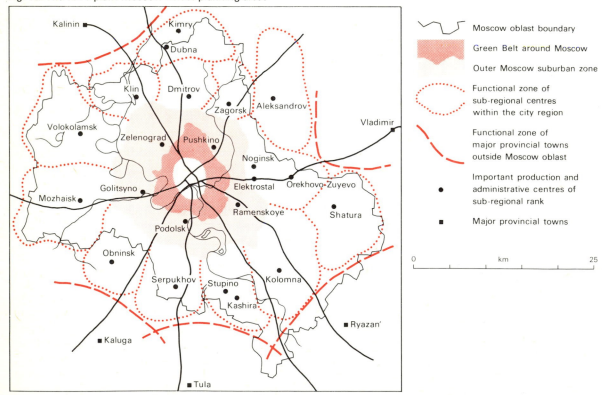

is to be tempered by transferring 'non-essential' (to Moscow) institutes and bureaux to major cities beyond Moscow *oblast*. Services are expected to engage 18 to 25 per cent of the working population by 1990, compared with only 11 to 19 per cent currently. Farms are to expand the cultivation of fruit, vegetables, and flowers.

The plan predicts a rise in the regional population from 12·8 million (1971) to 16–16·5 million by 1990 and to 18 million by 2000. Three zones are delimited for regional policy (Fig. 12): Moscow, a suburban ring (including the Forest Park Belt), and outer Moscow *oblast*. Quite distinct policies are proposed for each zone to redistribute population within the region: stabilization in the metropolis, a modest increase in the suburban ring, and rapid growth in outer Moscow *oblast* (Table 10).

The limitation of the population living within the Ring Motorway to 7·5 million may be very hard to accomplish in view of continued growth since 1971 at the rate of 100 000 persons annually, a figure which has remained remarkably constant since 1945, adding 3 million people in thirty years. In the short term, the population may well exceed the plan target but then decline as long-term factors take their toll: job decentralization, housing overspill, and the demographic effects of a currently ageing and low birth-rate population. Overall, the plan permits only a 10 per cent population increase in twenty years within 65 km of the Kremlin, while outer Moscow *oblast* will double in population (Tables 4 and 10).

Strict controls are being imposed by Moscow city and *oblast* authorities on employment location (requiring closures or relocation and controlling expansion or new development) and labour supply (giving or refusing permission for workers to change their place of residence). Metropolitan employment is to be stabilized at its present level: 4 million jobs. The number of commuters from the suburban ring will be reduced by 40 per cent to about 300 000 persons. Some industries will be removed from Moscow whilst some workers

Novosti Press Agency

Huge hothouses on *sovkhozy* near Moscow use thermal power-station heat to produce fresh food supplies

whose jobs remain in the metropolis will be permitted to take up residence there. More rigorous protection of the Forest Park Belt, enlarged from 1725 km² to 2750 km², should prevent further coalescence between Moscow and suburban towns. Built-up areas, already covering 400 km² or one-quarter of the smaller green belt of 1970, can be extended by no more than a further 100 km² to accommodate metropolitan overspill.

TABLE 10

Population changes projected by the second Moscow plan

	Population (thousands) 1971	1991	Percentage change
Moscow	7061	7500	+6·2
Outer metropolitan area (suburban ring)	3250	3850	+18·5
Outer Moscow *oblast*	2525	4650 to 5150	+84·2 to +104·0
Total	12 836	16 000 to 16 500	+24·6 to +28·5

The new ring accelerator at Serpukhov typifies policy to decentralize research to outer Moscow *oblast* towns

The limited development planned for the sub-urban ring includes only those activities essential to Moscow and is to be steered into outer towns such as Solnechnogorsk, Krasnoarmeisk, Ramenskoye, Golitsyno, and Istra, located 50–70 km from Moscow, once new towns in the Forest Park such as Zelenograd become self-contained.

The success of the containment policies in Moscow and the suburban ring depends upon substantial decentralization to (and the new growth of industries, research, and services, as well as an improved infrastructure in) outer Moscow *oblast*. The plan (Fig. 12) designates thirteen peripheral urban centres as future sub-regional nodes providing industries and services for rural hinterlands 35 km in radius. Their optimal population threshold for sustaining long-term growth is calculated to be 100 000. Only three zones at present contain towns of this size: Kolomna, Serpukhov, and the eastern zone containing three (Elektrostal, Noginsk, Orekhovo-Zuyevo). Four larger towns are scheduled for major expansion—Klin, Kolomna, Serpukhov, and Zagorsk—but the fastest growth is to occur in smaller centres, currently with 15–50 000 popu-lation, which are transport centres in rural areas with a ready labour supply: Volokolamsk, Mozh-aisk, Naro-Fominsk, Dmitrov, Dubna, and Shat-ura. Two minor 'conurbations' will be created as major sub-regional centres: Elektrostal/Noginsk and Kashira/Stupino. Growth is also planned in neighbouring Aleksandrov and Obninsk in co-operation respectively with the Vladimir and Kaluga *oblast* planning authorities.

A declining and dispersed rural population continues to pose serious planning difficulties, especially for servicing. The general plan calls for the elimination of 'town–country' differences by modernizing agriculture, providing hard-surfaced roads, and developing food-processing facilities. Long-term regrouping of the population from 7500 'rural' into 1800 (and, eventually, only 600–700) 'urban-type settlements' will assist the process.

Development beyond Moscow *oblast* is not, of course, a function of the general plan. The current 1971–5 Soviet Economic Plan is channelling industrial and tertiary activity into small or medium-sized towns and strengthening the attrac-tion of *oblast* administrative centres. Most small towns do not share in the development since they are too many and total growth is restricted. Rather, new activities are being concentrated in selected towns which command access to adequate rural and 'unoccupied' urban (mainly female) labour, and which are located at the junctions between the three ring routes around and the twelve radial routes from, Moscow. They include Rzhev and Nelidovo on the Riga route, Bologoye and Vyshny Volochok on the Leningrad radial, Murom and Arzamas on the Kazan' route. Such towns offer potentially good locations for energy- or material-intensive industries, engineering, research, and for providing regional services. The initial 'blueprint' for this strategy was devised by S.O.P.S. from research into the spatial patterns of labour supply and industrial structure in central European Russia. If the ring of outer Moscow *oblast* development centres prove to be successful, they may become models for decentralized economic growth throughout the city region in the 1980s.

Towards a model Communist metropolis

The general plan proposes far-reaching changes in the spatial organization and appearance of the Soviet capital. By the year 2000, Moscow will be a fundamentally decentralized metropolis within the Ring Motorway. Every citizen should be able to obtain all but the most specialized requirements with the minimum of travel within the zone of the city in which he or she resides: employment and all social services, shopping, culture, entertainment, sport, and access to open space. This is a mammoth task. Though less centralized than many Western capitals, Moscow, after years of *mikrorayon* planning, still concentrates a huge volume of jobs and services in the fairly specialized central and inner areas.

The framework for decentralization comprises eight planning zones (*planirovochnaya zona*): one central zone surrounded by seven outer ones (Fig. 13). Separated from each other by the Moskva river, wedges of open space, and new highways, they are to support projected populations in the 1990s of 450 000 to 1 100 000. Each zone will focus on a major zonal centre, an extensive precinct combining employment and services in the form of administration offices serving city, zonal, and other needs; hospitals; specialized stores, major cinemas, theatre, and restaurants; and a sports complex. Except for changes arising from urban

Fig. 13. The Moscow city plan 1971 : strategy for the 1990s

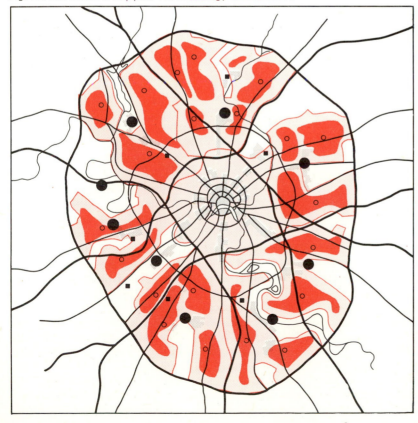

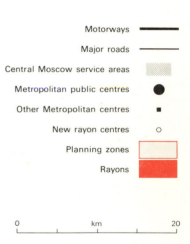

Motorways	▬▬▬
Major roads	──
Central Moscow service areas	�
Metropolitan public centres	●
Other Metropolitan centres	■
New rayon centres	○
Planning zones	
Rayons	

0   km   20

renewal, central Moscow already contains these facilities. Outer zones are broadly designed with a U shape, built-up urban 'prongs' projecting outwards towards the Ring Motorway, each separated by 'lobes' or 'wedges' of open space penetrating into the city from the Forest Park Belt.

A hierarchy of residential and functional sub-zones is planned within each planning zone. Three or four planning *rayons*, containing 200–400 000 people are to be formed, focusing upon new *rayon* centres located along major highways, as on Varshavskoye Chaussée in Chertanovo or on Leninsky Prospekt near Yugo-Zapadnaya. Such *rayon* centres will provide facilities for periodic use: shops selling consumer durables, restaurants, a children's theatre, a cinema, and a hotel. One planning *rayon* will comprise 5 to 10 residential districts, each housing 30 to 70 000 people. The residential district (*zhiloi rayon*) is the basic city planning unit. Serving groups of two or three of them are lower-order, district centres with shops offering everyday needs, schools, crèches, cinema, library, old people's home, hospital, and clinics. Though many district centres will be new, some will augment the facilities in existing *mikrorayon* centres.

Until the 1960s, Soviet city planning concerned itself primarily with housing and modest service provision at the lower *mikrorayon* and district levels. The new Moscow plan—symbolic of the increased emphasis in Soviet economic planning on expanding tertiary activities to levels appropriate to a highly industrialized urban society—outlines, for the first time, the location and spacing of a complete hierarchical system of service centres. These will double the *per capita* service provision. Six orders make up the hierarchy: (1) the primate metropolitan centre, essentially central Moscow, though extending beyond the Sadovoye Kol'tso; (2) nine general metropolitan public centres (*obshchegorodski obshchestvenny tsentr*) located in outer Moscow, sometimes in conjunction with (3) seven outer zonal centres; (4) twenty-one *rayon* centres; (5) sixty-six district centres; and (6) the existing *mikrorayon* centres. Though embryonic metropolitan-type centres (e.g. Kalinin Prospekt or the Dinamo-Sokol belt on Leningradsky Prospekt) and planning-zone-type centres (e.g. Degunino on Dmitrovskoye Chaussée) already exist, it has been the absence of such centres that has aggravated congestion in central Moscow. Most innovative is the creation of major service and administrative centres (especially orders 2, 3, and, partially, 4) of intermediate rank between the primate centre and the *mikrorayon* centres.

The projected role of the intermediate centres extends beyond improved local servicing. They will become the key recipients of decentralized office employment. The nine metropolitan public centres are to occupy attractive, almost 'out-of-town' sites in parkland, riverside, or other open spaces alongside, or within the outer planning zones (Fig. 13). By 1990 they are expected to employ 455 000 people mainly in specialized economic, social service, cultural, and infrastructural activities at a level of city, regional, Russian Republic, or even national importance. The Soviet television centre at Ostankino, *Gidproroyekt* offices at Sokol, and the new circus near the University are precursors of these general metropolitan centres. Some 370 000 people will continue to work in similar activities in central Moscow. The largest outer metropolitan centres will employ 40–110 000 people. Significantly, all are in currently 'non-industrial' wedges of the city. Complexes resembling Kalinin Prospekt in function (with administration, stores, services, restaurants, cinemas, and substantial amounts of housing) but different in design and scale, will be constructed in central areas of urban renewal along radial routes inside and outside the Sadovoye Kol'tso, for example around Komsomolsk, Kolkhoz, and Dobrynin Squares, or between Belorussky and Savelovsky railway termini.

Major changes in metropolitan land-uses will occur. Priority still goes to housing, mainly to increase living space for every Muscovite from 9 to 13·5 m² per head. Residential areas of 9- to 16-storey buildings will occupy progressively more farmland and wasteland to cover 64 200 ha by 1990, compared with 42 600 ha in 1971. Land-use planning will apply the zoning principle, segregating 'residential' from 'production' zones. Although this principle has governed new development since the 1930s, only limited enforcement has been attempted in areas of pre-Revolutionary vintage. Since 1971 the operation of three parallel processes has been achieving zoning throughout the city (Fig. 14). First, the demolition of all pre-1930 quarters (except historic monuments) in inner and central Moscow (especially Zamoskvorech'ye) is eliminating incompatible land-uses and industry and reducing the concentration of administrative, service, and research functions. The comprehensive redevelopment of these areas will increase parkland, especially along the Moskva and Yauza rivers, create broad avenues, and provide more high-rise housing immediately beyond the Sadovoye Kol'tso. Secondly, the closure of factories in inner south-eastern and western Moscow is freeing land for services, sport,

46

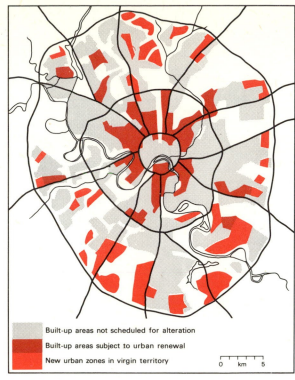

Fig. 14. Urban development and renewal in Moscow city during the Ninth Five Year Plan, 1971–5

and housing. Thirdly, massive construction will continue on virgin sites in outer Moscow. The major problem here will be to improve timing. On past experience, service provision normally lags 2 to 3 years, and the completion of integral *mikrorayon* facilities 4 to 8 years, behind the housing programme. Divided responsibilities and different construction techniques for housing and service buildings are to blame.

The new Moscow plan designates sixty-six production zones, dispersed among existing and new sites. These will house present, new, or relocated manufacturing, utilities, planning and research bureaux, communal services, warehouses, garages, and building enterprises. The success in decentralizing employment depends upon the mobility of these functions. Movement is no problem for most tertiary and quaternary functions; new premises are highly prized. Least mobile is manufacturing because plants are usually large and administered by R.S.F.S.R. or Soviet ministries. Smaller enterprises of city importance, administered by an arm of *Mossoviet*, are more amenable to being moved. Between 1971 and 1990 about sixty such plants in inner Moscow will be closed, thirty-three new plants opened in outer Moscow, whilst only nineteen are to be modern-

ized *in situ*. The rapid growth of a widening range of services offers greater opportunities for dispersion. Labour, too, is mobile. To move people, especially skilled personnel, from one zone to another is far easier and cheaper than moving functions, especially since apartments are highly uniform throughout the city.

Nevertheless, it is recognized that daily, interzone commuting will continue into the 1990s on a substantial, though much reduced, scale. Most planning zones should achieve labour : job ratios within 10 per cent either way, so avoiding cross-commuting between zones. Even so, 425 000 commuters will pour daily into central Moscow, another 125 000 into the west to make up the large labour deficits there. The majority will travel from south-west Moscow or the green belt.

The new Moscow plan proposes far-reaching improvements in metropolitan transport. Existing *magistrali* (Prospekts, Chaussées) are to be widened, linked up, and provided with two-level interchanges to form a complete system of radial 'urban clearways' from the Bul'varnoye Kol'tso to the Ring Motorway. Top priority goes to an intermediate ring highway in inner Moscow where truck traffic will remain heaviest. The most radical change, however, is scheduled for the 1980s when the first Soviet inter-city motorways will be opened. Five urban motorways (from ten radial directions) are projected to cross the Soviet

Fig. 15. The Moscow metro

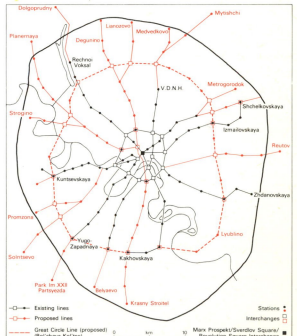

capital, bypassing and forming a 'motorway box' enclosing the central and older inner areas (Fig. 13), and facilitating rapid communications between all planning zones.

The extension of the metro (Fig. 15) will confirm its supremacy as the major form of urban passenger transport. Five new radial lines are planned to connect the Circle Line around central Moscow with the outer residential areas currently poorly served by transport: Chertanovo (south), Gagarin (south-west), Mnevniki (west) and Tushino (north-west), Beskudnikovo-Lianozovo (north), and Perovo (east). Existing and new radial lines will be extended to future districts near the Ring Motorway, even beyond it to Mytishchi, Reutov, Lyubertsy, and Solntsevo to relieve suburban *elektrichka* or buses in carrying commuters from the Forest Park. The greatest innovation, and truly the masterstroke of the plan, is the projected *Bol'shaya Kol'tsevaya Liniya*, an outer 'Great Circle Metro Line' linking all the general metropolitan, zonal, and some *rayon* office and service centres and providing a mass-transit passenger service transverse to all radial road, metro, and suburban railway routes with which it will have interchanges.

These improvements, particularly the ring routes, are long overdue. Central Moscow will be relieved of traffic congestion, noise and fumes. Yet development must keep abreast of need. Inevitably greater densities of truck traffic will circulate among more dispersed production zones, carrying a vastly increased volume of goods destined for distribution through the wider network of service centres. The modest 150 000 private cars registered in Moscow and the suburban ring in 1970 will swell to 500 000 by 1980, probably one million in the 1990s. The plan

provides for car parks, garages, petrol stations and servicing points (there were only sixteen in Moscow in 1970) but these are places where future congestion may occur. Although the authorities have the power to regulate car sales, consumer demand exceeds supply and may well be influenced by how quickly the extended metro system serves the new outer residential areas. Yet, for the average Muscovite, it is the metro that will open up maximum accessibility to each zone of the metropolis.

The proposed metro and motorway systems put their seal on continuation of the radial/ring pattern as the dominant force shaping the future of the city region. That pattern has roots deep in Russian history, beginning with the ring system of defensive monasteries on the radial river and road routes to and from medieval Moscow (Fig. 8). A tantalizing question remains. Will the much improved transport network assist the achievement of a decentralized metropolis or will it encourage inertia on the part of authorities and labour alike and so sustain higher levels of interzone movement? In any event, the fulfilment of the new general plan will give every Muscovite in the twenty-first century just cause to look back and proudly echo the words of the poet Mayakovsky:

> Moskva belokamennaya,
> Moskva kamnekrasnaya,
>   svegda
>   Byla mnie,
>   Mila i prekrasna.*

*Moscow of white stone,
    Moscow of red stone,
  Always
      Was to me,
          Dear and beautiful.

Further Work

Without knowledge of the Russian language, the student must be content to read generally about the Moscow region in basic textbooks. A wide range of general geography texts have been written by J. P. Cole, W. G. East, R. A. French, D. J. M. Hooson, P. Lydolph, R. E. H. Mellor and W. H. Parker. Further, there are two important texts for the serious student of planning: P. J. Bernard, *Planning in the Soviet Union* (1966) and A. Nove, *The Soviet Economy* (1965). A map is indispensable, even for the non-visitor to Moscow. By far the most useful is the Falk plan *Moskva* which gives names in English, German, and

Russian but which like all other Moscow maps is not to scale: the inner and outer areas are particularly distorted.

More material is available to the student with Russian linguistic expertise. Major sources are: *Tsentral'ny Rayon* (1973) in the economic regions series; Yu. G. Saushkin, *Moskva: Geograficheskaya Kharakteristika* (1964); *Stroitel'stvo i Arkhitektura Moskvy*, 7–8, 1971; G. B. Polyak and E. V. Sofronova, *General'ny Plan i Byudzhet Moskvy* (1973); and *Puti Razvitiya Malykh i Srednikh Gorodov Tsentral'nykh Ekonomicheskikh Rayonov SSSR* (1967).